BLOOMSBURY NEEDLEPOINT

MELINDA COSS

BLOOMSBURY NEEDLEPOINT

FROM THE TAPESTRIES AT CHARLESTON FARMHOUSE

WITH CHARTS OF DESIGNS BY
DUNCAN GRANT, VANESSA BELL & ROGER FRY

A BULFINCH PRESS BOOK
LITTLE, BROWN and COMPANY
BOSTON · TORONTO · LONDON

For Justine, Juliette and Robin.
I saved the best for you.

First North American Edition

First published in Great Britain by Ebury Press,
an imprint of Random House UK Limited.

Editorial direction: Lewis Esson Publishing, London
Art direction: Andrew Gossett MSTD
Design: Studio Gossett
Photography: Pia Tryde
Copy editing and chapter introductions: John Wainwright
Needlepoint charts: Colin Salmon and Tim Pearce

ISBN 0-8212-1919-7
Library of Congress Catalog Card Number 92-53271
Library of Congress Cataloging-in-Publication information
is available.

Bulfinch Press is an imprint and trademark of
Little, Brown and Company (Inc.)

Published simultaneously in Canada by
Little, Brown & Company (Canada) Limited

PRINTED IN ITALY

CONTENTS

FOREWORD

by Angelica Garnett

I have pleasure in introducing a book whose purpose is to encourage and promote the interest felt in the designs of my parents, Vanessa Bell and Duncan Grant. It is a fact that these designs, many of them invented as people sometimes say 'merely' for pleasure, have the immediate effect of arousing our desire to do the same. I cannot help wondering how much this has to do with the spirit in which they were conceived, which was – I think – very close to that of a child making its first visual experiments. Not of course exactly the same, because both artists were highly versed in the technique of design, but not only had they freed themselves from any preoccupation on this score – that is to say they had found their own voices, their own personalities – but they had rediscovered the same purity of spirit with which a child makes its drawings simply for the fun of it.

This is a kind of second childhood that can only be achieved by those who have made the choice of giving themselves wholly to their ideal or vision; but I think it is one we all envy and would give a lot to experience. Here the opportunity is handed to us by Melinda Coss in such a way as to save us all the hard work of calculation and knowing what to buy. Having got the materials, we can sit by the fire or under the apple tree in the garden dreaming of Vanessa or Ethel Grant doing the same thing. Then, after weeks or even months of delightfully dogged persistence, we may produce a piece of work worthy – it is to be hoped – of its inspiration.

Questions of the greatest complexity are involved in this adventure, the most relevant being that of fidelity. While the impulse to do such a thing must be fundamentally due to a desire to create something of our own, it is essential to realize that we have chosen to do it through the medium of another person and, in order to retain the special attraction of his or her idea, we must be faithful to that idea. Our faith involves ourselves as well, since our choice was the result of the sympathy we had for the original. As Melinda Coss says in her Preface – and as is the case in any human relationship – we must be prepared to give up any predilection or prejudices we may have, to do justice to the task we have knowingly set ourselves – and this may not always be easy.

In any design there are three elements: form, colour and texture. In changing one the whole is affected; just as, in a piece of music, if we change a bassoon for a 'cello, the effect is utterly different. Sometimes we cannot find the right coloured wool, and have to substitute another – and in doing so we sometimes unexpectedly improve matters! But this is the kind of accident we cannot rely on, and has more to do with the development of our own taste than the work in hand. The most important ingredient is sympathy: if we cannot, for any reason, repeat the design to the letter, then we must do so in the right spirit.

In recalling my parents at work, it is the spirit which comes to mind. An idea, which might occur to them at any odd moment – in a train or on the top of a bus in Piccadilly – would be noted down on a scrap of paper – or, with luck, in a tiny sketch book – to emerge in the studio, very likely in the more relaxed moments when the main work of the day was over. Then they would start doodling on a larger piece of paper, dreaming around the initial idea to produce one drawing after another – usually with a 6B pencil. Duncan would often continue to do this while talking, with a drink at his elbow, thus divided between two delightful occupations. When the bell rang for supper the design might be put away and forgotten – there was a drawer in the studio knee-deep in such drawings – or on the following day it might be transferred to a piece of paper that had some relation to the finished size. The drawing might now be very lightly sketched in charcoal, and colour added. Duncan tended to work fast, Vanessa slowly. Whereas, during the course of a morning, he might produce something spirited, lively and full of colour, so that at lunch time we would all exclaim at the amount he had achieved, Vanessa would still be tracing – slowing and dreamily – a large simple shape, with as yet only one or two colours. She would have difficulty in justifying, even to herself, the depth of her concentration, but it was fascinating to watch the trance-like gestures, and guess at the dreams which prompted them.

Occasionally, Ethel Grant, Duncan's mother – who worked so many of their designs – came to stay at Charleston, bringing with her a cloth hold-all containing embroidery wool in finely graded colours, and the piece of work in progress. It was always known as her cross-stitch, regardless of any more exact term, and the different wools or stitches she used where chosen to reflect the feeling of the design, and for no other reason. This was done in consultation with Vanesssa and Duncan, who themselves had only the most elementary idea of embroidery stitches, and were often appreciative of Mrs Grant's inspiration. When necessary, as it sometimes proved to be, she was always ready to unpick rows of painstaking stitches, her only desire being to catch the spirit of the design as faithfully as possible. Although faded – in the same way that her embroidery has now lost some of its intensity – her beauty as an old lady was still impressive. As she sat drawing out her long lengths of wool, Vanessa and Duncan would stand at their easels painting her portrait. What seems to have disappeared from the world is the ability to make time for these things. The opportunity to atone for this is one of the joys we are offered in this excellent book.

ABOUT CHARLESTON FARMHOUSE

by Christopher Naylor

Charleston is today the last complete example of the domestic decorative art of Vanessa Bell and Duncan Grant. The house and collection are in the care of the Charleston Trust, a registered charity founded to preserve Charleston for posterity.

Of the many friends and relatives who made Charleston an important artistic focus, Duncan Grant was the last to survive. Grant lived at Charleston on and off for over 60 years, but the house was always on a rented basis, the property of the Firle Estate. By the time of his death in 1978, aged 93, the house was falling into worsening disrepair: Charleston, always known as somewhere cold and lacking in creature comforts, now suffered a leaking roof and serious rising damp.

Swift action was imperative; after Grant's death an additional cause for worry was the Farmhouse's appearance on the market as a desirable property 'in need of some re-decoration'. Thanks to the founding generosity of the families concerned, principally Quentin and Anne Olivier Bell, and Angelica Garnett, initial funding was secured to launch the Charleston Trust and to acquire the freehold; at the same time the families kindly donated back to the Trust almost all the contents of the house. The task of re-creating Charleston as it had been became therefore a realistic objective.

The first stage of the restoration was the re-establishing of a basic structure secure from the elements: a new roof, new floors in many areas, and indeed in some entire new walls, requiring the careful removal of the unique 'wallpapers' which had been hand-stencilled in situ. A new heating system had to be installed, to provide the correct environmental conditions for long-term preservation. Expert conservators were enlisted to address the specialist needs of the collection itself – the needlepoints and textiles, the ceramics, the painted furniture, the paintings and murals.

Considerable private donations, from the United States as well as from Great Britain, had to be secured to fund the programme, in addition to public grant aid.

Outside the gardens too had suffered. The exciting coloured borders of the past had given way to grass: past layouts and planting schemes had therefore to be researched, through examination of paintings and diaries, and indeed excavation of the walled garden itself.

In early 1986 the garden was replanted, and in the summer of 1986 Charleston opened to the public for the first time, despite several outstanding projects. An ongoing conservation programme was established to care for the contents while continuing to display them to the public in a domestic setting.

Charleston is now open to the public from April to October for four afternoons each week (Wednesdays, Thursdays, Saturdays and Sundays) though this is subject to change.

In its continuing care for the collection the Charleston Trust remains almost entirely dependent on donations and subscriptions, receiving only very limited public grant aid. The Trust is assisted by a support body, the 'Friends of Charleston' (and its sister body in the United States, the 'American Friends of Charleston'), whose members subscribe on an annual basis and in return receive the twice-yearly Charleston Magazine, and other benefits.

Charleston Farmhouse, Nr. Firle, Lewes, East Sussex BN8 6LL; 0323 811 265/626

INTRODUCTION

by Jane Dunn

Charleston Farmhouse has been part of the Sussex landscape for more than 300 years. Situated about 6 miles east of Lewes, near Firle, it has survived modestly as the house of various tenant farmers, as a boarding house and, for a short time, a makeshift sty and stable. Largely north-facing, cold and neglected, and in need of a new tenant, it would have been difficult to imagine, in the grim war year of 1916, that it was about to be woken from a sleep.

During the next half century, pallor and greyness gave way to an explosion of image and colour: obscurity was replaced with a reputation across continents as Charleston became known as the country retreat primarily of the painters Duncan Grant and Vanessa Bell and her family, but also of their friends – painters, writers and philosophers: the Bloomsbury Group.

To those who visited it, the name Charleston became synonymous with stimulating talk, good food and wine, time and peace for work amongst others hard at work. In the colours, the paintings and layers of decorative detail of the rooms, there existed an enchantment of place which left few untouched.

Vanessa was eventually to die there in 1961. Duncan lived on, the house falling into greater disrepair than he did, almost until his death in 1978, at the age of 93. Charleston was by then in a sorry state, water, frost and vermin having made their depredations on the fabrics, the needlework, the paintings, the murals, the very structure of the house. Expensive words like protection, repair, restoration were being muttered. Eventually The Charleston Trust was set up and the daunting work of fund raising and emergency repairs was begun.

Now more than a decade later, a fortune gone, and a lifetime of man- and woman-hours spent, the house sits resplendent in its riotously blooming garden; its rooms translucent with meticulously matched paints, restored wallpapers and textiles, the retouched murals. Colour, pattern, image, some so familiar and others compellingly strange, meet one at the entrance to every room . . . paintings abound . . . and the pieces of needlepoint, faded with age and use, are focal points of colour and light – on a wall or floor, framing a mirror, giving distinction to a bench or chair.

There are many strands – artistic, personal and historic – which make up the phenomenon of Charleston. From there they spread out again into the full creative lives these people lived, largely at this Sussex farmhouse and in their London houses amongst the garden squares of Bloomsbury.

The historic part of the story really starts with the Stephen family in early 1904, newly orphaned by the death of their father, Sir Leslie Stephen. Vanessa, the oldest, was 24; Thoby, down from Cambridge, was 23; Virginia just 22 and Adrian 20. Vanessa and Virginia had already determined to be painter and writer respectively, and Vanessa particularly was determined to leave their unhappy past behind by moving the family as far as was decently possible from the house in which they had grown up, in socially acceptable Kensington.

Thus it was that she chose the district of Bloomsbury. Rather raffish, with no family friends to trouble them: it was only just respectable. For the two sisters particularly it was the beginning of the life of which they had long plotted and dreamed. A life pared down to essentials – work, friendship, freedom. And the house Vanessa had chosen to rent, 46 Gordon Square, seemed to make these ideals possible at last.

She wrote in a memoir years later about what this move had meant to her; 'It was exhilarating to have left the

Vanessa Bell

house in which had been so much gloom and depression, to have come to these white walls, large windows opening on to trees and lawns, to have one's own rooms, be master of one's own time.'

It was to this large, airy, even chilly, house that Thoby's Cambridge friends came to weekly Thursday Evenings, with cocoa and biscuits offered around. This weekly focus of friends, good talk and cocoa, was the germ of the 'Bloomsbury Group'. Because Bloomsbury was not a commune, however, but rather a tendency, a mutual philosophy of work and life, there is some confusion as to who were its members.

The core of that circle, whose influence ranged over art, literature and economics, originally consisted of Vanessa, Virginia, Thoby (until his death) and Adrian Stephen; Lytton Strachey, biographer; Leonard Woolf, political writer and socialist activist; Clive Bell, art critic; Maynard Keynes, economist; Molly and Desmond MacCarthy, literary journalists; Saxon Sydney-Turner, cerebral civil servant; Roger Fry, art critic and painter; and the artist Duncan Grant. The novelist E. M. Forster philosophically belonged there too. And all, apart from Thoby who died young, were to spend some time at Charleston, in varying degrees caught in its spell.

In the airy rooms of Gordon Square, Virginia wrote and rewrote what was to become her first novel *The Voyage Out*. Both sisters took their vocations seriously; hard work was bred into them from their parents and they intended always to be professional, and to earn a living from their art. Vanessa, setting out in her chosen profession was painting a few commissioned portraits and experimenting to find her own style, less realistic than her teachers, pared down to essentials of form and colour.

Having found themselves as young women, outsiders,

ill-at-ease in conventional society, and having cast off most of their more distant family connections, Vanessa and Virginia sought in this fellowship of like-minded friends an alternative society, a proxy family, with themselves at the very centre. The support and affection of the group gave them the confidence to experiment in their different arts. They could strike out, Vanessa into her own interpretation of Post-Impressionism, much vilified as it was, and Virginia into a new form of novel writing, subjective, non-narrative, charting a 'stream of consciousness'.

Their brother Thoby's death at 26 of typhoid was quickly followed by Vanessa's marriage to Clive Bell, one of his Cambridge friends and one of their number. She had evaded marriage until she was nearly 28, perilously late for a young woman then. (Virginia, with even more reluctance than her sister, finally married Leonard Woolf, another of their number, in 1912 when she was 30.)

1904 had been the year of personal liberation for the Stephen sisters with their move to Bloomsbury, and a life of work – with friends of their own persuasion. But 1910 was to be a more universally significant year for all the artists and writers of the group.

Quentin Bell, Vanessa and Clive Bell's second son was born that summer, not in itself at the time a momentous event, but he was an unwitting cause of his mother being drawn into greater intimacy with the painter Roger Fry – and subsequently of Roger's energetic entry to their world. Vanessa was desperately concerned over the state of her sickly baby and Roger's quick sympathy and good sense forged an immediate bond. She then introduced him to the young painter Duncan Grant and there was established an artistic sympathy and collaboration which was to enrich all their lives.

Meanwhile the literary sister, Virginia Stephen (she was yet to become Woolf), had not been idle. At the end of 1910, she rented a small semi-detached cottage in Firle in Sussex near the sea, and christened it Little Talland House, after her family's summer house in St. Ives in Cornwall. This was the beginning of the establishment of 'Bloomsbury-by-the-Sea', centred eventually on the sisters' country houses, Charleston and Monk's House at Rodmell, just 5 miles away. For the rest of their lives Vanessa Bell and Virginia Woolf, their husbands, friends and family, were to leave the squares of Bloomsbury to come to this part of Sussex for holidays. They were eventually to settle there permanently during the Second World War.

Then, in the last months of 1910, there occurred a seismic event which was to shake the art world in London and spread its after-shocks into society at large. Roger Fry organized the first Post-Impressionist exhibition in London and introduced to general view the shockingly uncouth paintings of Van Gogh, Gauguin, Cézanne, Matisse and Picasso. To a public used to art which was largely realistic, narrative and sentimental, these canvases were a moral and artistic outrage.

Roger Fry was attacked by the Establishment as either a charlatan or a madman, but the young English painters gathered around him, none more moved than Vanessa Bell: 'That autumn of 1910 is to me a time when everything seemed springing to new life - a time when all was a sizzle of excitement, new relationships, new ideas, different and intense emotions all seemed crowding into one's life.'

Although she was becoming more enamoured of Roger himself, it was the excitement of the art which seemed to extend its own energy and liberation into every area of her life. The vulgar exuberance of colour, the abandonment of realistic draughtsmanship and of sentimental baggage, the very lack of politeness and pretence, were all an authorization of her own artistic and personal freedom.

Virginia also recognized the sea-change that seemed to be marked by this mutinous exhibition, 'On or about December, 1910, human character changed' she wrote some fourteen years later in an essay on the challenges facing the modern novelist. And she was to try and incorporate the lessons of the Post-Impressionists in her own writing of fiction, 'Literature was suffering from a plethora of old clothes. Cézanne and Picasso had shown the way; writers should fling representation to the winds and follow suit.'

Two years later in 1912 the Second Post-Impressionist Exhibition was mounted, again by Roger Fry with close collaboration, and pictures, from Vanessa and Duncan. It was a mixed bag of a show, some dazzling paintings from the French with Matisse and Cézanne and some cubist work from Picasso mixed in with a varied and rather derivative collection of English paintings and some out-of-place Russian symbolists. More scorn was heaped on their heads . . . the excitement was intense.

Roger Fry was an influential art critic and an extraordinary friend and enthusiast who encouraged and promoted the work of the younger artists gathered around him under his banner of Post-Impressionism. His love affair with Vanessa during these years, and his respect for her and her work, was to enrich her life immeasurably and maintain her place in his affections until he died.

His vision of Post-Impressionism which had such a profound effect on Duncan and Vanessa's work – and Clive Bell too who formalized it in his book *Art* – was that it appealed to the imagination through the interaction of

form and colour, not through any imitation of nature. Sentimentality and narrative detail were abandoned for something more immediate and much closer to the emotional truth.

These were the artistic and personal influences which were to find expression in the walls and fabrics of Charleston – even in the very way that life was lived there. They attempted to get to the point of things, what really mattered, and do away with unnecessary emotional baggage and demands of outmoded convention.

A further significant move was Roger Fry's establishment of the Omega Workshops in Bloomsbury's Grafton Street in 1913. He, Vanessa and Duncan were co-directors of an enterprise which was intended to encourage young artists by displaying their decorative skills in the spirit of Post-Impressionism, and to provide them with a common workshop, a showroom and marketplace.

He was a practical man as well as a visionary and he knew how difficult it was for artists, painting in this controversial style, to earn a living from their work and he hoped that Omega would provide additional income and employment for them. But the didactic visionary in Roger Fry's nature was not subdued for long; he felt personally involved in a crusade against English good taste and had the messianic hope that through the Omega he would infiltrate Post-Impressionism into the hearts and homes of the interior-decorating classes and thereby 'make art possible in England'.

Vanessa was closely involved with Omega design and production, particularly at the beginning. She produced designs for fabrics, rugs and clothes. She painted screens, pottery and an animal mural for a Post-Impressionist nursery. The Omega was open to commission from

members of the public for almost any decorative detail from stained-glass windows and mosaic floors to marquetry trays and hand-painted teapots. Byzantine mosaics and African and pre-Colombian art were greatly admired by Roger Fry and his enthusiasm infected Duncan and Vanessa (see Duncan's brilliant *Giraffe* design dating from this time and reproduced in this book).

The Omeganic style was irreverent, witty and exhilarating, but occasionally – if consistently adhered to – it could be overpowering. Virginia Woolf, slightly jealous of the enthusiasm and creative collaboration of the artists at this time, wrote an amused and deflationary aside to her sister who had designed some of the clothes which their new sister-in-law Karin Costelloe, step-daughter of Bernard Berenson, had had the courage to wear in public:

'My God! What clothes you are responsible for! Karin's clothes wrenched my eyes from the sockets – a skirt barred with reds and yellows of the violent kind, a pea-green blouse on top, with a gaudy handkerchief on her head, supposed to be the very boldest taste. I shall retire into dove colour and old lavender, with a lace collar and lawn wristlets.'

The experiment of the Omega was to last less than 6 years, but Duncan and Vanessa were to carry on and develop many of the decorative ideas in private commissions and on the walls and furnishings of their own houses.

The next momentous date was October of 1916. It was then that Charleston was plucked from obscurity to become the embodiment of a way of life and art which reflected, in Raymond Mortimer's phrase, 'the varied richness of a cultured intelligence'.

The property was discovered first by Leonard Woolf who was staying that summer with Virginia in their

nearby rented villa, Asheham House. Virginia had been wanting to lure her sister back to her side in Sussex. Vanessa was far too distant, living as she did at Wissett Lodge in Suffolk, keeping house, caring for her two young sons and the painter Duncan Grant with his friend David 'Bunny' Garnett. As conscientious objectors during the First World War, they were attempting to farm there.

Virginia's letter to her described Charleston's hidden qualities: 'It is about a mile from Firle, on that little path that leads under the downs. It has a charming garden, with a pond, and fruit trees, and vegetables, all now rather run wild, but you could make it lovely. The house is very nice, with large rooms, and one room with big windows fit for a studio . . . There is a w.c. and a bathroom, but the bath only has cold water. The house wants doing up – and the wallpapers are awful. But it sounds a most attractive place – and 4 miles from us.'

Vanessa did move her large rackety household from Suffolk to Charleston and the transformation of the place, although slow at first, was ready to begin. First came the injection of life; children calling out, fires lit in the main rooms, the smell of cooking, visitors from London. Those first three years in this large cold house with the barest facilities were grim. There were wartime shortages of food and fuel, the house was remote down a rutted track, and the burden of feeding and keeping this large household going fell to Vanessa.

But wherever she lived, Vanessa always created her own unique environment, making do with what was at hand, dyeing fabric, painting walls, decorating furniture and shutters. The decoration of the interior of Charleston, which became so much a part of that house's character and charm, evolved over the decades. Largely the work of both Duncan and Vanessa, the designs and colour of

Charleston's interiors went on changing with the enthusiasms and experiments of the many artists who lived and worked there.

The house was never subject to a grand design scheme, although a distinctive palette of colour ran through various rooms and decorations, bringing a unified visual sense to the whole. And always there were the paintings, largely by the artists themselves and their immediate friends and colleagues, although when Clive Bell's French pictures arrived at the end of the Thirties there was a Picasso, a Vlaminck and a Matisse jostling for space on the walls along with the rest.

Furniture, some painted, some plain, some barely better than firewood, some of rare age and quality, added to the visual richness of the place. They would happily mix heirlooms with pieces bought in local junk shops, or with furniture manufactured and decorated for the Omega Workshops. All made a sometimes surprising – but always satisfying – whole with the chalky wash of the walls and the exuberant gods and goddesses, the fruit, flowers and more abstract patterns of croquet hoops and crosshatching, which framed fireplace, window and door.

And then there were the textiles. The loose covers and curtains, often made by Vanessa, sometimes in fabric printed with their own designs, are a distinctive part of the pleasure and feeling of simple comfortableness of the house. But most remarkable of all is Charleston's wonderful needlepoint. Here fine art and applied art most nearly meet. The painters' designs were translated triumphantly through the inspired needlework of Duncan Grant's mother Ethel (although Vanessa and occasionally Virginia did some canvaswork too) into beautiful cushion covers, frames for mirrors, rugs, firescreens, wall hangings, stool and chair covers. You will find most of them in this book, designed largely by Duncan or Vanessa, although the lovely *Peacock* of Roger Fry is also included.

Charleston was primarily created by Vanessa as a place for artists to work, specifically where Duncan Grant, whom she loved, would want to work. She hoped to bind him to her with the compelling atmosphere of the place. It was one of ease and industry, and organic growth. As the garden, fields and trees changed with the years and seasons, so too the house itself was never static in its reflection of the creative energy of its inhabitants.

The garden was an integral part of the seduction of the place. The main section lay to the north of the house, walled in old brick, overgrown and neglected. It was reclaimed over the years and new plantings and features were added as Vanessa particularly became increasingly interested in gardening. Twenty years after her first viewing of the property, she could write, 'The garden is now a mass of flowers & as gay as possible with holly hocks & sweet peas & zinnias – tobacco & stocks smell strong in the evening. I often wander about in it at odd moments for the pleasure of the sights & smells.'

The pond to the east of the house, although outside the colourful compass of the walled garden, was another imaginative focus. Large, willow-fringed and full of duckweed, it was the scene for all sorts of adventures, for fallings-in and mad-cap schemes for clearing. It was also a cool and restful spot for sitting out – as Virginia wistfully imagined the scene, 'Nessa is at Charleston. They will have the windows open; perhaps even sit by the pond. She will think This is what I have made by years of unknown work – my sons, my daughter. She will be perfectly content (as I suppose).'

Although they employed a gardener, guests would happily settle down to weed or dig when necessary:

Duncan Grant

Maynard Keynes was known for his demon weeding and the length of his visits could be measured by the inches of cleared path.

Structural improvements to the house were gradually instituted, an inadequate heating and hot water system in 1919, electricity eventually in 1933. But the most important addition was the construction of a large studio in 1925 on the garden front, designed by Vanessa, Duncan and Roger Fry, to give as much space as possible for the least cost.

Despite life at Charleston being centred on the painters' needs, the writers amongst their friends found the peace and routine of the house conducive to their art too. Clive Bell wrote sections of his famous tracts, *Civilisation* and *Old Friends* there. Even more notably, the economist Maynard Keynes wrote most of his famous polemic *The Economic Consequences of the Peace* in what became known as Maynard's Bedroom, with its wonderful 'Morpheus' bedhead, during the summer of 1919 when the house was still in its most inhospitable phase.

Virginia, the most famous writer of the group, although a frequent and appreciative visitor, was never to spend any length of time there. She always had her own country house nearby, first Asheham and then Monk's House, but she feared that her own household did not have the magnetic appeal that Charleston seemed to radiate.

The relationship of these formidable sisters is also the story of Charleston. From an early age they formed 'a very close conspiracy' against the demands and expectations of the male members of their family and of society in general. But such closeness also implied competition, and from the beginning these women divided the worlds of art and experience into two. Each presided, sometimes jealously, over her domain. Vanessa claimed painting as her own, Virginia writing; Vanessa took sexuality and motherhood, Virginia intellectuality and imagination.

They offered each other emotional and financial support, mutual artistic inspiration, admiration and affection. The whole was based on shared experiences, family loyalty and a resolute dedication to their art. Virginia wrote virtually every day of her life and in a memoir reflected, 'I feel that by writing I am doing what is far more necessary than anything else.' Vanessa, having experienced both marriage and motherhood, returned time and again to the opinion that 'Art is the only thing; the lasting thing, though the others [marriage and motherhood] are splendid.'

Work was at the centre of the sisters' lives and each had a distinctive influence on the art of the other. Virginia wondered whether her fiction was not more truly biography – certainly her central figure, more often than not, was inspired by her need to explore her fascination with Vanessa.

Pacific, civilized, from rooms with views and views into rooms, Vanessa's and Virginia's work shared a certain perspective. Virginia's writing would make her sister at times want to paint the images which sprang from the page. Virginia's physical beauty also inspired a series of portraits by Vanessa which capture, even in those without facial detail, a concentrated stillness and the richness of her internal life. They directly collaborated in The Hogarth Press, the publishing house started by Leonard and Virginia Woolf, which published Virginia's works clothed in exuberant Bell dust jackets. And together they produced an illustrated *Kew Gardens* where Virginia's limpid prose is almost overwhelmed by the organic profusion of Vanessa's leaves and flowers, waves, hoops and dashes.

Childless, Virginia was free to channel all her energies into her work and her friendships. But there was always the example of her sister, fertile, loved by husband, lovers (Roger Fry reluctantly gave way to Duncan Grant) and children (Julian, Quentin and Angelica). In her bleaker moments she would look at her life and see it as an arid thing compared with Vanessa's riches. And nowhere did she feel this more keenly than at Charleston.

This house in its heyday expressed triumphantly Vanessa's human and artistic qualities. In its evolving, ubiquitous decorations, its informality and atmosphere of creative industry, Charleston was a living work of art – some might claim Vanessa's masterpiece. Friends queued to be invited, drawn by the stimulation of the company and the restorative ease of their surroundings.

Although she needed servants to help her run the place, Vanessa carried the final responsibility for everything: the hiring, humouring and firing of servants; the managing of the family's finances; the care, welfare and education of the children; the organization of a large household (often swollen with guests who might stay for weeks at a time) and all the provisions from firewood to pheasants that this entailed. The structural improvement and additions to Charleston; the decorations and furnishings of the house; the planting and maintenance of the garden: all fell ultimately to Vanessa.

There was variable moral support, together with suggestions and some financial help from the men in her life: from Duncan Grant, from Clive Bell, and at different times from Roger Fry and Maynard Keynes. It was Vanessa who carried the whole edifice and made it work. But she had her vocation too, her art, the demands of which had to be answered if she was to function happily – or even remain sane.

Virginia, sitting writing in her more modest Monk's House, would imagine Vanessa at Charleston, 'humming & booming & flourishing over the hill', like some great source of energy. It amazed her to hear from her sister occasional expressions of despair at how melancholic she sometimes felt, having spread herself so thinly, never finding enough time to paint. Only to Roger Fry was Vanessa able to reveal the rawness of these fears, writing from Charleston awaiting the birth of Angelica at the end of 1918: 'Oh dear if you knew how difficult I find it now to keep my head above domestic worries . . . I can't paint you see which is the one infallible refuge from such things.'

But these failures of heart were only temporary. The work did go on and Virginia was an appreciative and generous patron to the artists at Charleston. As her fame increased and she made more money, she commissioned paintings, furniture and decorative work from Vanessa and Duncan to enliven her London rooms and those of Monk's House.

Tiles featuring the Godrevy lighthouse at St. Ives (the original in *To the Lighthouse*) were designed and painted by Vanessa and used to surround the fireplace in Virginia's new bedroom at Monk's House. They painted for her too a dining table and chairs, their backs distinguished with the angular monogram V W, one initial arrow-sharp upon the other.

Virginia could be intimidated by her sister's unerring eye and sense of colour and when she boldly chose an apple green colour for the walls of her sitting room she felt sure the Charlestonians (i.e. Vanessa) would ridicule it. Vanessa probably did; she had a low opinion anyway of the charms of Monk's House compared to Charleston, considering it a 'queer poky jumbled cottage', but it was only an expression of the lifelong sisterly rivalry which meant each felt a certain unease when the other trespassed into her domain.

As Vanessa grew older, Charleston was to feature increasingly as the focus of her life. The visits to London became less frequent. The deaths of Roger Fry and then, in 1937, of her beloved elder son Julian in the Spanish Civil War made her retreat further. The Second World War confined her still more but she accepted these restrictions philosophically, listening to the bulletins on the radio and writing to Duncan who was on a war-artists' commission in Plymouth, where he was enjoying himself enormously and had lost his heart, he joked, to the magnificent Admiral of the Fleet.

Charleston once more changed to accommodate the needs of those who lived there. To counteract the food shortages, Vanessa planned to grow more vegetables and breed chickens to eat. Her studio in Fitzroy Square in Bloomsbury was bombed and some of her paintings destroyed. She greeted this news with equanimity, she could always paint some more she said. Petrol was short and so she had to combine visiting Virginia at Rodmell with going into Lewes shopping.

The war was fought over their heads. Heavy German bombers blotted out the sun as they droned their way to blitz London. Invasion was a very real possibility. There were dog fights over Charleston in the Sussex skies. Planes were shot down. Virginia wrote in her diary of a German plane coming down near the village and 'the country people "stomped" the heads of the 4 dead Germans into the earth': primitive emotions lay close beneath a thin veneer of civilization.

Then came the phone call from the Woolfs' gardener on 28 March 1941 telling Vanessa that Virginia could not be found, Leonard was searching for her and she was feared drowned. This was the personal tragedy that was added to the darkest days of the war.

Life continued in its daily routine, sadder and more grim. Vanessa and Duncan were still painting. During the war the murals commissioned by the Bishop of Chichester for Berwick Church, just 2 miles distant, were being

planned and painted on large panels back at Charleston, 'the house is chaotic,' Vanessa declared, 'and all a dither with Christianity.'

War ended and the life of the house opened out a little. Angelica had married David Garnett and now her four daughters were welcome visitors, returning a youthful energy to the house as they ran from kitchen to garden, posing for Duncan and Vanessa in the studio and munching digestive biscuits while listening to *Mrs Dale's Diary* on the wireless. Then when Quentin married Olivier Popham in 1952 there were more grandchildren to come and stay adding their childish voices to the sounds and voices and memories already imprinted into the fabric of the walls.

In its meticulous restoration, Charleston remarkably has retained a lived-in feel; a chair still sags as if a bottom has only just vacated it, the beds bear the indentation of bodies just up from comfortable sleep. The house has a powerful presence even now: everything in it expresses the vivid personalities of those who transformed it with their appetite for life and a sensual pleasure in the appearance of things.

Virginia Woolf, incomparable in her ability to transfix an image with a phrase, conjures up the life that one imagines inhabits Charleston still:

'Charleston is as usual [she wrote in the summer of 1922]. One hears Clive shouting in the garden before one arrives. Nessa emerges from the great variegated quilt of asters & artichokes; not very cordial; a little absent-minded. Clive bursts out of his shirt; sits square in his chair and bubbles. Then Duncan drifts in, also vague, absent-minded, & incredibly wrapped round with yellow waistcoats, spotted ties, & old blue stained painting jackets. His trousers have to be hitched up constantly. He rumples his hair. However I can't help thinking that we grow in cordiality, instead of drifting out of sight . . .'

AUTHOR'S PREFACE

I open this preface with a tribute to Charleston and to the dedicated people who work there today. The house is, quite simply, a time capsule and the unique creative talents of those members of the Bloomsbury Group who lived and worked there are evident in its every corner. The furniture and paintings, restored with such meticulous care, appear undisturbed in the environment for which they were intended. The personal items, paints and writing equipment give a valuable insight into the characters of a group of extraordinary people who called the house home. For those of you who have never visited Charleston, I urge you to do so.

I am, primarily, a knitwear designer, and as such I often find myself confronted with versions of my own designs which have been altered to the taste of the person who has knitted them up. There have been occasions when subtly-shaded pink wools have been replaced with violent candyfloss-coloured acrylics, and pieces of patterns have been left out or put in with absolutely no thought for the idea behind the original design. People are entitled to their personal preferences, but that doesn't stop the designer's urge to set fire to the offending item or to shout violent abuse at the person who took it upon themselves to 'improve' the design. I have been aware of these feelings throughout the compilation of this book and I hope that the artists whose work I have attempted to reproduce will understand my limitations and look on me kindly.

Bloomsbury Needlepoint has been an exercise in self restraint and personal discipline, two virtues which I have never possessed and which have only been demonstrated thanks to the constant supervision of Christopher Naylor at Charleston who hasn't allowed me to get away with a thing. For the first time I have not been free to interpret my own ideas, could not state different shades when I felt they were appropriate, and have had to admire the subtle

changes time has made to the Charleston needlepoints while working the remakes to the original colours.

Take the Day-Bed, for example (*see* page 58). It is quite clear to me, and to all who have seen this piece, that black is contrasted with chocolate brown, and that a square abstract black image appears behind the central motif. This black square, to my eyes, gives the design a new dimension, and while the back of the needlepoint confirms that the chocolate isn't brown at all, but simply an unevenly faded black, I argue that the new colourings are appropriate to their surroundings and, indeed, an improvement on the original. Perhaps Duncan Grant is still working the design? Many of the images used for needlepoints were changed and changed again during the painting and stitching process. Since nobody knows the artists' original intentions, I present you with the truth – and nothing but – according to the areas of canvas untouched by time and wear.

Then there are the stitch details. Were the stitches really supposed to change direction mid-stream. Were the varied lengths of background stitches intended, or was someone in a hurry to complete the piece? Was an odd colour introduced simply because of a shortage of available yarns? Only the designers themselves could say.

What is unquestionable is the sheer joy and spontaneity of the designs, a factor which gives my strict approach a curious irony. I have wondered, on several occasions, while counting the stitches on a faded photograph, if Duncan and Vanessa might find the painstaking reproduction of these needlepoints an amusing scenario.

Having told you how difficult the book has been to write, I must now tell you how pleased I am that I have been forced to take such a strict approach. Each piece has been a revelation. Riots of unexpected colour have jumped out from the faded canvases and brought the images exploding back to life. The 'Shell' Cushion (*see* page 32) and the chairseats (*see* pages 79-86), selected by me for inclusion because of their clear graphic images, contain the most vivid of colour combinations – an assortment of contrasts that no one could have convinced me would work until I saw the completed pieces. The boldness of the designs and the use of optical illusion in items such as the Mirror Frame are extraordinary. I would doubt that such an approach has ever been applied to needlepoint before.

As a good deal of time has passed since the original pieces were made, it has been impossible to match colours and canvases exactly. In some cases rough hessian was used as a base and I have replaced this with antique finish double-mesh canvas. To match the colours as closely as possible I have used a combination of Paterna tapestry wools and Appleton's crewel wools, the colour ranges of both being extensive, but neither of which could, on its own, satisfy the original specifications. In some examples the designs were sketched on the canvases in ink and while many of these marks were ignored during the stitching, the show-through of ink lines form such an intrinsic part of the image that they had to be indicated on the charts. On other occasions I have worked these lines as shadows, using a slightly darker shade. On the Two Fishes Rug (*see* page 112), the sketch marks were so bold that I have applied them in stem stitch over the finished needlepoint.

If you have ever attempted a needlepoint you will appreciate that time, perhaps even more than skill, is the greatest resource. Because of time, or the lack of it, I have not been able to remake all the designs that I have charted. The charts, however, are accurate and worked to the same scale as the original pieces. Although it has been impossible to estimate the quantities of yarn required for those pieces I have not made up, the appropriate yarns are listed alongside the chart. You should also note that for the Vase of Flowers Chairseat Cover (*see* page 79), I have used half-cross stitch where the original piece was produced in cross stitch. You can rectify this by doubling the quantities of yarn required and producing the piece in cross stitch. If you choose to do this, use one less strand of yarn than the strands quoted.

Some of the designs are taken from original paintings and it is questionable whether the pieces were ever actually produced as needlepoints. I chose to include the abstract Vanessa Bell Rug for its wonderful colours. It may, however, have been designed for a table top.

There are numerous people who deserve the 'author' credit as much as I do. Top of my list has to be Christopher Naylor and the team at Charleston, whom I have driven insane over the last months. Then there are my stitchers: warmest thanks to Mary Baker, who not only stitched the Shell Cushion, Abstract-patterned Cushion and Mirror Frame with amazing skill, but must have worked twenty-four hours a day to do so. Mrs Gibson, thank you for the Giraffe design, and thanks to Sylvia Eade for the Vase of Flowers Chairseat Cover and the Vanessa Bell Rug. Also to Carolyn Palmer, who stitched the Two Fishes Rug and the Bowl of Fruit Chairseat Cover in record time, and Mrs Bryant, who is responsible for the wonderful Peacock canvas. Thanks also to Virginia Nicholson, who spent days researching the whereabouts of rare needlepoints. Thanks to the Courtauld Institute, where many of the original paintings can be seen, and of course to Angelica and Henrietta Garnett for their kindness in allowing me to reproduce the work of their family.

Finally, thanks to my editors Hilary Arnold, Lewis Esson, and John Wainwright, the designer Andrew Gossett, the photographer Pia Tryde, and all the team at Century/Ebury, who have been an absolute joy to work with.

THE GARDEN ROOM

Prior to 1917 the main sitting room at Charleston was known as the Drawing Room. However, within a year of Vanessa Bell moving in (September 1916) it acquired its present name – the Garden Room – and went on to become one of the most beautiful creations in the house. Situated on the ground floor, between Clive Bell's study and Vanessa's bedroom and at the front right-hand corner of the house, the room has a view through foliage over the pond and across the fields to Tilton, and French windows opening on to the walled garden at the side of the house.

Enjoying an abundance of natural light, the Garden Room has provided the setting for several important portraits over the years. Notable among these are Duncan Grant's painting of Vanessa (c. 1917), which hangs in the National Portrait Gallery in London; Grant's *Girl at the piano* (1940), which can be seen at the Tate, and Vanessa's *Evening in the country*, a large composition showing Duncan Grant and Clive Bell sitting by lamplight after dinner.

Although it often served as a place for painting, the Garden Room was always, first and foremost, a family sitting room and a place for entertaining numerous friends and acquaintances. Several memorable and diverse events took place here including, for example, Desmond MacCarthy, author, critic and at the time literary editor of the *New Statesman*, reading and explaining T.S. Eliot's *The Waste Land* to Duncan Grant and Clive Bell and, on a more poignant note, Vanessa telling her 18-year-old daughter Angelica, in the summer of 1937, that Duncan Grant was her natural father.

Working from designs by Roger Fry, 'Bunny' Garnett had constructed the fireplace that forms the focal point of the room within a year of moving in (1917), and *c.* 1928 Duncan Grant added the striking overmantel decoration of two bare-breasted women supporting an inset mirror with painted oval frame. (When the mirror broke some years later, Grant painted an oval of yachts in its place; and later still the basket of flowers which survives to this day.) However, apart from a repeat stencil pattern on either side of the chimney breast, the walls remained plain until 1945, when the room was redecorated by Vanessa and Duncan. Employing colours and stencilled motifs sympathetic to the eclectic collection in the room, they created the harmonious scheme that survives (albeit restored) today.

Of the many functional and decorative artefacts in the room, those particularly worthy of note include two needlepoint cushion covers designed by Vanessa Bell (for making up, *see* page 117) and a pelmet and curtains

Above: *The three-fold, painted wooden screen that stands between the back of an upholstered chair and the door to the Garden Room was originally in Duncan Grant's studio at 8 Fitzroy Street, London. Grant decorated the front of the screen with distressed colour and floral and circular motifs* c. *1934, but did not paint the back of it until* c. *1955.*

Left: *The abstract-patterned, needlepoint cushion cover, which can also be seen in the chair above, was designed by Vanessa Bell* c. *1932, and worked by Ethel Grant, Duncan Grant's mother.*

Right: *A collection of well-thumbed, French and English art periodicals from the 1920s sit on a tiled table-top designed by Quentin Bell during the 1950s.*

Far right: *The needlepoint 'Shell' cushion cover, designed by Vanessa Bell* c. *1925, was worked by Ethel Grant. Its original bright colours have faded rather pleasingly over time. The curtains behind are made up from the* Grapes *fabric designed in 1931 by Duncan Grant for Allan Walton Ltd.*

made from the *Grapes* fabric designed in 1931 by Duncan Grant. The furniture includes a French work table and an English card table with floral marquetry inlay (both 19th-century). Two ceramic Italian pots and a 19th-century French lion stand on the mantelshelf, while a triple-fold wooden screen and a log box display Grant's talents as a decorative painter.

However, it is the paintings in the Garden Room that perhaps best reflect the occupants of the house and their interests and inspirations. In the early years several pictures by Rouault, Matisse, Vlaminck, Gris and Picasso hung here, but were eventually sold. However, Quentin Bell's copy of Picasso's *Pots et citron* (1908), and Vanessa's copy of Vlaminck's *Poissy-le-Pont* (1947) both hang here now. Other present pictures include *Flowers* (c. 1925), by Matthew Smith and *46 Gordon Square* (c. 1909-10), by Vanessa Bell. To the left of the fireplace is the highly regarded *Self portrait* (c. 1958), by Vanessa Bell, capturing her critical sensibility and the sadness of her later years, having lost many close relatives and friends.

A blue, yellow and white ceramic Italian pot, one of a pair, sits on the mantelshelf in the Garden Room. The overmantel decoration behind was painted by Duncan Grant c. 1928. The kneeling woman, together with her 'sister' on the other side, now supports a painted basket of flowers – Grant's replacement for the original inset mirror that broke many years ago.

The log box, which stands in front of the fire-surround in the Garden Room, was painted c. 1917 by Duncan Grant. One of the earliest decorated objects in the house, it displays angel musicians and dancers on all four sides.

ABSTRACT– PATTERNED CUSHION

This abstract-patterned cushion was designed by Vanessa Bell and produced around 1932. The mixture of stitches employed give it a wonderful textured finish, although one stitch in particular presented a problem during the remaking process. A large question-mark hung over the identity of the putty-coloured background stitch, which I eventually interpreted using oblique slav (see page 116). It would seem that the original stitch was chosen for speedy coverage. On close inspection, it appears that some areas were produced at a speedier rate than others!

The original design was stitched on a hessian background, and the pale lemon panels appear to have been produced on a finer mesh and then sewn in. To reproduce this effect I have varied the thickness of the crewel yarns, and while the coverage may not appear to be sufficient in some areas, I believe that the attendant show-through of antique mesh adds character in harmony with Vanessa Bell's original concept.

WORKING THE DESIGN

Once you have prepared the canvas (*see* page 117), mount it on a frame (*see* page 115). Work the main body of the design using the stitches, strands and yarns indicated in the chart and key shown *right*. With the exception of black Ap993 and turquoise Ap520/5, each colour is worked in one stitch type throughout. Embroider the black stem and leaf design over the finished needlepoint using stem stitch (*see* page 116).

BLOCKING AND MAKING UP

Block and finish your completed needlepoint (*see* page 117). Once the blocked work is completely dry, make it up into a cushion (*see* page 117). Note that the original cushion is backed in a chestnut-brown wool fabric and edged with black curtain braid. Also note that the beauty of this cushion lies not only in its appearance, but also in its size, and therefore comfort. I would suggest that a large feather pillow inside the finished cover will reproduce the required effect.

MATERIALS

Tapestry yarns in the colours and quantities shown *right*.
Antique finish, 10-mesh double canvas. 80cm (31½in) by 64cm (25in).
Size 18 tapestry needle.
Tools and materials for preparing the canvas (*see* page 114), for blocking (*see* page 117) and for making up (*see* page 117).
Large feather pillow.

The design measures 69.8cm (27½in) by 53.3cm (21in).

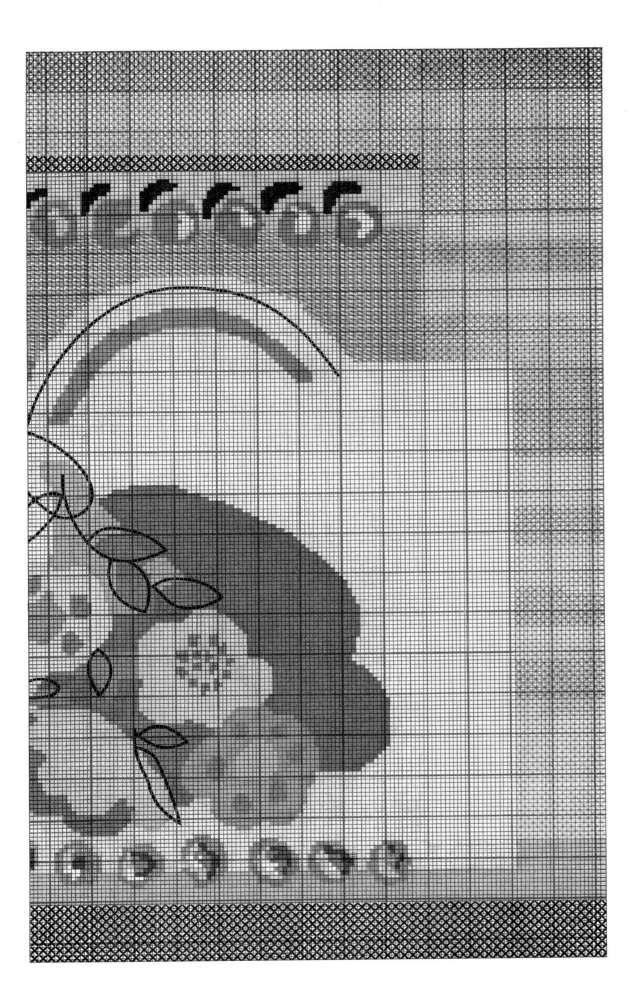

YARNS

Ap980/5	40gm	(1.41oz)	
Ap980/1	25gm	(0.88oz)	
Ap980/7	50gm	(1.76oz)	
Ap930/3*	10gm	(0.35oz)	
Ap930/1*	5gm	(0.18oz)	
Ap200/9*	10gm	(0.35oz)	
Ap140/4	5gm	(0.18oz)	
Ap750/1	15gm	(0.53oz)	
Ap120/5*	10gm	(0.35oz)	
Ap120/2	12gm	(0.42oz)	
Ap300/3*	5gm	(0.18oz)	
Ap760/3	10gm	(0.35oz)	
Ap620/5	5gm	(0.18oz)	
Ap470/5	5gm	(0.18oz)	
Ap550/5	5gm	(0.18oz)	
Ap690/2	5gm	(0.18oz)	
Ap870/2	25gm	(0.88oz)	
Ap840/3	25gm	(0.88oz)	
Ap840/2	30gm	(1.06oz)	
Ap640/7*	5gm	(0.18oz)	
Ap350/4	5gm	(0.18oz)	
Ap350/2	5gm	(0.18oz)	
Ap420/7**	5gm	(0.18oz)	
Ap520/5***	5gm	(0.18oz)	
Ap150/4	5gm	(0.18oz)	
Ap150/2	5gm	(0.18oz)	
Ap740/7*	10gm	(0.35oz)	
Ap993	15gm	(0.53oz)	
Ap960/5	25gm	(0.88oz)	
Ap991	5gm	(0.18oz)	

Ap = Appleton's crewel wool.
Use three strands throughout for all above,
except:
* Use two strands.
** Use one strand.
*** Use three strands for half-cross,
one strand for petit point.

THE SHELL CUSHION

It was the Shell Cushion, designed in 1925 by Vanessa Bell, that provided my inspiration to produce a book on Bloomsbury needlepoint. Ironically, I was initially attracted by the chalky appearance and subtle effect of the faded colours. On taking the cushion apart, however, the true colours, unexposed to the ageing effects of light and everyday use, emerged – along with new insight into the feeling behind the Bloomsbury designs. Vanessa Bell's bold approach to the original bright colours, coupled with the strong abstract image, provided an exciting and rewarding revelation.

MATERIALS

Tapestry yarns in the colours and quantities shown *right*.

Antique finish, 10-mesh double canvas. 71cm (28in) by 60cm (23½in).

Size 18 tapestry needle.

Equipment for preparing the canvas (*see* page 114), for blocking (*see* page 117) and for making up (*see* page 117).

The design measures 61cm (24in) by 49.5cm (19½in)

WORKING THE DESIGN

Once you have prepared the canvas (*see* page 114), mount it on a frame (*see* page 115). Using two strands of yarn throughout, follow the chart on the *right* and work the main body of the design in half-cross stitch. Work the details by embroidering over the finished needlepoint: stem stitch (*see* page 116) and one strand of black yarn for the black stems; back stitch and one strand of Pa870 yarn for the criss-cross pattern in the middle of the flowers.

BLOCKING AND MAKING UP

Block and finish your completed needlepoint (*see* page 117). Once the blocked work is thoroughly dry, make it up into a cushion (*see* page 117).

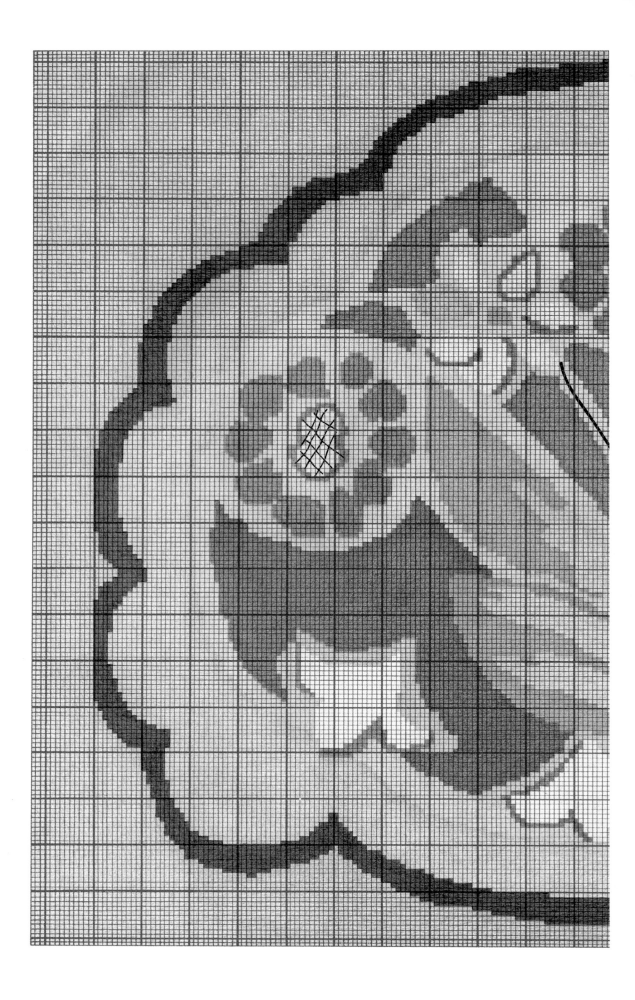

YARNS

Pa643	12gm	(0.42oz)	■
Pa644	45gm	(1.59oz)	□
Pa654	9gm	(0.32oz)	□
PaD546	6gm	(0.21oz)	▨
Pa604	9gm	(0.32oz)	□
Pa743	3gm	(0.12oz)	□
Pa701	3gm	(0.12oz)	▨
Pa854	9gm	(0.32oz)	■
Pa461	12gm	(0.42oz)	▨
Pa320	16gm	(0.56oz)	▨
PaD127	12gm	(0.42oz)	□
Pa945	6gm	(0.21oz)	□
Pa934	9gm	(0.32oz)	□
Pa220	21gm	(0.74oz)	■
Pa212	40gm	(1.41oz)	□
Pa203	5gm	(0.18oz)	□
PaD133	72gm	(2.54oz)	▨

Pa = Paterna tapestry yarn.
Use two strands throughout for the main
body of the design.

GIRAFFE STOOL COVER

This wonderful Duncan Grant design was produced in 1913 for a stool cover, or possibly a chair seat. The original painting is in the Courtauld Institute in London. Since I could not establish the whereabouts of a stitched version, I have matched the yarn colours to those in the painting and worked the entire design – to the size of the artwork – in half-cross stitch on 10-mesh canvas. It is possible that the original was worked in cross stitch. However, I feel this would prove too dense for 10-mesh. On the other hand, if you wish to enlarge the design you could work it in cross stitch on a larger mesh canvas.

The Giraffe design is closely related to Grant's 'Cat on a Cabbage', and the frail, half-worked canvas for the latter can be seen at Charleston, along with its original painting. In order to make a closer match with 'Cat on a Cabbage', it is possible Grant intended that there should be more foliage in the surround of the Giraffe needlepoint – more than he included in the painting. Nevertheless, I have reproduced only what I have seen, since I do not wish to risk misinterpreting what I consider to be a brilliant piece of design.

MATERIALS

Tapestry yarns in the colours and quantities shown *right*.

Antique finish, 10-mesh double canvas. 56cm (22in) by 55cm (21½in).

Size 18 tapestry needle.

Equipment for preparing the canvas (*see* page 114), for blocking (*see* page 117) and for making up (*see* page 117).

WORKING THE DESIGN

Once you have prepared the canvas (*see* page 114), mount it on a frame (*see* page 115). Using two strands of yarn throughout, follow the chart on the *right* and work the entire design in half-cross stitch (*see* page 115).

BLOCKING AND MAKING UP

Block and finish your completed needlepoint (*see* page 117). Once the work is thoroughly dry, make it up into a cushion (*see* page 117) or a chair-seat (*see* page 117), or simply frame it and hang it on the wall.

The design measures 45.7cm (18in) by 44.5cm (17½in)

YARNS

Pa870	12gm	(0.42oz)	■
Pa871	15gm	(0.53oz)	■
Pa872	11gm	(0.39oz)	■
Pa541	30gm	(1.06oz)	■
Pa603	15gm	(0.53oz)	■
Pa604	6gm	(0.21oz)	■
PaD531	11gm	(0.39oz)	■
Pa694	6gm	(0.21oz)	■
Pa724	12gm	(0.42oz)	■
Pa725	3gm	(0.11oz)	□
Pa960	6gm	(0.21oz)	■
Pa961	9gm	(0.32oz)	■
Pa963	6gm	(0.21oz)	■
Pa204	51gm	(1.80oz)	■
Pa261	6gm	(0.21oz)	□

Pa = Paterna tapestry yarn.
Use two strands throughout.

VANESSA BELL'S BEDROOM

From 1916-1939, apart from a brief period in December 1918 when she moved into Duncan Grant's Bedroom for the birth of their daughter Angelica, Vanessa Bell's bedroom was situated on the first floor of Charleston. However, as part of the major structural alterations carried out on the house on the eve of the Second World War, the old dairy and larder on the ground floor was converted into a new bedroom for her and her old bedroom became Clive Bell's library (The Library).

In the old dairy the source of natural light was limited to one small window facing the walled garden. However, as part of the alterations the window was removed and replaced by French windows. As a result there was a substantial increase in the amount of light entering the new bedroom. The French windows also gave Vanessa direct access to the garden, and it is no coincidence that, under her supervision, and driven by her and Duncan Grant's enthusiasm for the project, an intense program of cultivation began soon after she moved in to the room and continued for the duration of the Second World War. Indeed, by the end of the war so many new shrubs and flowers had been planted that Vanessa wrote to her daughter complaining 'one can hardly walk down the paths for the plants that get in the way'.

In addition to the French windows, a pair of large double-doors providing direct access to The Studio were installed at one end of Vanessa's new bedroom. From 1925-1939 Vanessa had shared The Studio with Duncan Grant and done much of her work there. In 1939, however, a new studio was also established for Vanessa on

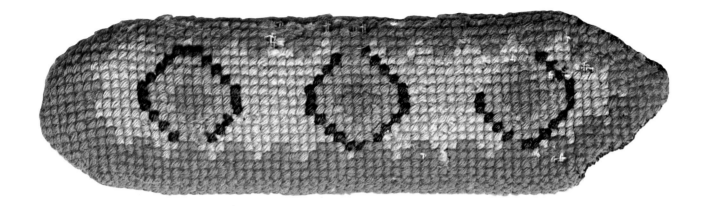

the second floor of the house, and the main Studio became increasingly Duncan Grant's territory thereafter.

Other improvements made to the bedroom during its conversion included the laying down of wooden floorboards, which replaced the dairy's original brick floor, and the installation of a washbasin and bath, the latter in a corner and usually concealed by a folding screen.

As part of the decoration of the new room, the walls, ceiling, doors and architraves were painted in plain white or pale pastel colours that contrasted with the furniture. To the left of the double-doors leading to The Studio there is a tall cupboard (which originally housed a folding bed), the panelled doors of which are embellished with striking yellow circle motifs on a brown background. It was decorated by Vanessa c. 1917. The bath panel decoration was completed by Duncan Grant c. 1945; another cupboard was painted by Angelica Bell, Vanessa's daughter, at some point during the late 1930s; and a marble-topped washstand beside the washbasin was decorated by Vanessa, c. 1917, with subtly distressed pale red and green paintwork and an abstract vase of flowers.

Other items of furniture include Vanessa's bed, by Heal & Son, which is covered with a Turkish embroidery bedspread bought on a trip to Broussa in 1911, a 19th-century chest of drawers, which stands next to the bed, a 19th-century French drop-fronted secretaire, which served as Vanessa's writing desk, and various period side chairs.

The curtain that can be seen in the bedroom today is a copy made by Laura Ashley (1987) of the *White* fabric designed by Vanessa for the Omega workshops in 1913.

Notable among the many artefacts and personal possessions in the room are a charming ink blotter cover designed by Vanessa Bell and worked in needlepoint, and a needlepoint spectacle case, possibly designed by her sister Virginia Woolf. A mirror with an embroidered frame, designed by Duncan Grant c. 1940, hangs over the washbasin. On the top shelf of the desk is a bust of Vanessa's daughter, Angelica, by Quentin Bell c. 1938, and on the windowsill are two imitation Han bronze pots.

The paintings that hang in the room are almost all of Vanessa's family. Three are by Vanessa herself; two being studies in oil of Julian Bell as a baby, painted in 1908, and the other a *Portrait of Henrietta* (c. 1957), Vanessa's grand-daughter. All the other paintings are by Duncan Grant. They include a *Self portrait*, painted c. 1910 at Fitzroy Square, London; *Lessons in the orchard* (1917), which shows Julian and Quentin Bell with their nurse, Mabel Selwood; *Quentin Bell* and *Julian Bell writing*, painted c. 1919 and c. 1928 respectively; *The Spanish dancer* (1931), and *Angelica Bell as Ellen Terry*, a pastel inscribed 'To V.B. from D.G. 1935' showing Vanessa's daughter Angelica dressed for her part in Virginia Woolf's play *Freshwater*. There is also a picture of the *Charleston pond in winter* (painted Christmas, 1950), inscribed 'To VB from DG'.

Above: *A 19th-century French provincial side chair, re-covered in a reproduction of Duncan Grant's* Grapes *fabric (designed in 1931), stands in front of the open French windows in Vanessa Bell's bedroom.*

Above left: *Vanessa's spectacle case was worked in cross-stitch needlepoint. Some attribute the design to Vanessa herself, while others credit it to her sister Virginia Woolf who, together with her husband Leonard, was a regular visitor to Charlston. If the case was Virginia's, it might have been used as a pen holder rather than as a spectacle case.*

Right: *A 19th-century, French drop-front secretaire served as Vanessa Bell's writing desk in her bedroom. The simple, floral-patterned fabric cover of her ink blotter, which sits at the front of the desk, was designed by Vanessa and worked in half-cross stitch needlepoint. A box camera in one of the open compartments reveals that her interests in the visual arts encompassed photography as well as painting and design.*

Right: *A view from the walled garden, through the open French windows into Vanessa Bell's bedroom. Her bed, by Heal & Son, is covered with a Turkish embroidery bedspread bought in Broussa in 1911. The painting above the bed –* Portrait of Henrietta *(c. 1957), by Vanessa Bell – is of her granddaughter and was painted at Charleston.*

Left: *The mirror with a wool embroidered frame that hangs above the wash basin in Vanessa Bell's bedroom was designed by Duncan Grant and worked by his aunt Violet McNeil c. 1940.*

Below: *The marble-topped washstand to the left of the basin was decorated by Vanessa c. 1917, within a year of her moving into the house.*

SPECTACLE CASE

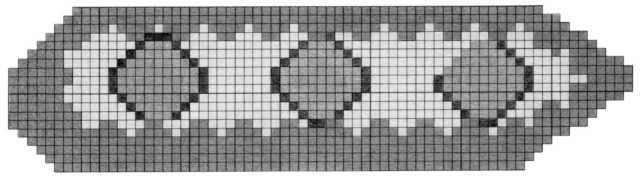

While some credit this design to Vanessa Bell, others suggest that Virginia Woolf originated it. I, in turn, would question the fact that the finished piece was designed to hold spectacles since, unless they were very tiny, wire-framed half-moons, they would have been too big to fit in it. My somewhat romantic theory is that this case was designed by Virginia Woolf and intended to hold her pen. If you wish your finished piece to serve this purpose, then it's a simple matter of reproducing the case to its original size (as shown by the chart). If, on the other hand, you wish to produce a case which will accommodate your spectacles, I have included instructions right on how to increase the size of the original design.

MATERIALS

Tapestry yarns in the colours and quantities shown *right*.
Antique finish, 10-mesh double canvas. 28cm (11in) by 23cm (9in).
Size 18 tapestry needle.
Equipment for preparing the canvas (*see page 114*), for blocking (*see page 117*) and for making up (*see page 117*).
Fawn-coloured silk lining material, 28cm (11in) by 23cm (9in).
Snap fastener.

YARNS

Pa861	*12gm*	*(0.42oz)*	▨
Pa731	*6gm*	*(0.21oz)*	▨
Pa734	*12gm*	*(0.42oz)*	☐
Pa962	*6gm*	*(0.21oz)*	▨
Pa221	*3gm*	*(0.12oz)*	▨

Pa = Paterna tapestry yarn.
Use two strands throughout.

The design measures:
Front – 14cm (5½in) by 4.4cm (1¾in).
Back – 16.5cm (6½in) by 5.1cm (2in).

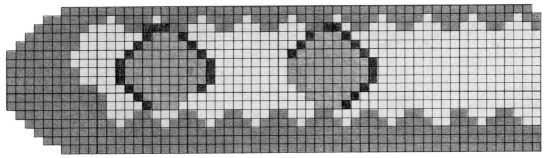

WORKING THE DESIGN

Once you have prepared the canvas (*see* page 114), mount it on a frame (*see* page 115). If you intend to make up the finished needlepoint as a pen holder, use two strands of yarn throughout and, following the charts above, work the entire design in cross stitch. If, on the other hand, you intend to make up the finished needlepoint as a spectacle case, work the design as for the pen holder, but increase the size of the rust-coloured background area until it is slightly larger than the outline size of your spectacles. Do bear in mind that you will need to buy additional yarn if you intend to increase the size of the design from that shown here.

BLOCKING AND MAKING UP

Block and finish your completed needlepoint (*see* page 117). Once the blocked work is thoroughly dry, cut around the front and back leaving a 1.9cm (¾in) seam allowance. Then cut the lining material to the same size. Take the needlepoint and fold the allowance back to the wrong side of the work, then baste it into place. Take the lining material and simply press under the allowance. With the wrong sides of the lining and needlepoint together, overcast around the edges to attach the lining to the canvas. Place the lined front and back together, with the two needlepoint halves facing outward. Using rust-coloured yarn and an overcast stitch, seam the

sides together through both thicknesses of canvas. Finally, sew a small snap fastener on to the underside of the point, right in the middle, with its second half in the corresponding position on the front of the case.

45

THE CHARLESTON MIRROR

This Duncan Grant design was produced in 1940 and is, without reservation, my personal favourite from the collection. Every time I look at it something new comes to light. By cleverly swapping colours from border to border, to create shadow and depth, the artist has created an image that provides a fascinating optical illusion. When working the piece, my advice is to follow the chart very carefully, because just when you imagine you are working a repeat panel the colours and the number of stitches will change . . . and very few things are worse than having to unpick needlepoint!

MATERIALS

Tapestry yarns in the colours and quantities shown *below*.

White, 12-mesh single interlock canvas. 73cm (28½in) by 64cm (25in).

Size 18 tapestry needle.

Equipment for preparing the canvas (*see* page 114), for blocking (*see* page 117) and for making up (*see* page 117).

Sheet of cardboard, 62.3cm (24½in) by 53.3cm (21in).

Sheet of hardboard, 62.3cm (24½in) by 53.3cm (21in).

Craft knife.

Rubber-based adhesive.

Carpet tape.

Sheet of hardboard, same size as canvas.

Mirror, 62.3cm (24½in) by 51.3cm (20½in).

Picture hooks (optional).

YARNS

PaD123	*60gm*	*(2.12oz)*	⬛
Ap930/3	*10gm*	*(0.35oz)*	⬛
Pa433	*12gm*	*(0.42oz)*	⬛
Pa455	*84gm*	*(2.96oz)*	⬜
Pa713	*12gm*	*(0.42oz)*	⬜
Pa672	*24gm*	*(0.85oz)*	⬜
Pa645	*24gm*	*(0.85oz)*	⬜
Pa513	*6gm*	*(0.21oz)*	⬛
Ap820/5	*10gm*	*(0.35oz)*	⬛
Pa201	*36gm*	*(1.27oz)*	⬛
Pa220	*18gm*	*(0.63oz)*	⬛

Pa = Paterna tapestry yarn.
Use two strands throughout.

Ap = Appleton's crewel wool.
Use three strands throughout.

WORKING THE DESIGN

Once you have prepared the canvas (*see* page 114), mount it on a frame (*see* page 115). Using two or three strands of yarn (as specified *below left*), and following the chart on the following page, work the main body of the design in half-cross stitch (*see* page 115). Work the black lines by embroidering over the finished needlepoint in stem stitch (*see* page 116), using two strands of yarn.

BLOCKING AND MAKING UP

Block and finish your completed needlepoint (*see* page 117). Once the blocked work is thoroughly dry, it is ready to make up into a mirror frame. Cut a sheet of cardboard to the same size as the needlepoint, using a craft knife to cut out the square in the middle. Trim away the waste canvas in the middle of the needlepoint. Leave a 5cm (2in) allowance all around, slitting diagonally into the corners so that it can be bent back over the cardboard frame. Stick the cardboard to the back of the needlepoint, using a rubber-based adhesive. Place the mirror behind the needlepoint frame and secure it to the cardboard back with strips of carpet tape. Finally, trim a sheet of hardboard to the size of the frame and stick it on to the back of the mirror with an adhesive suitable for glass. (If desired, small picture hooks can be carefully inserted into the back of the hardboard.)

The design measures 62.3cm (24½in) by 53.3cm (21in)

47

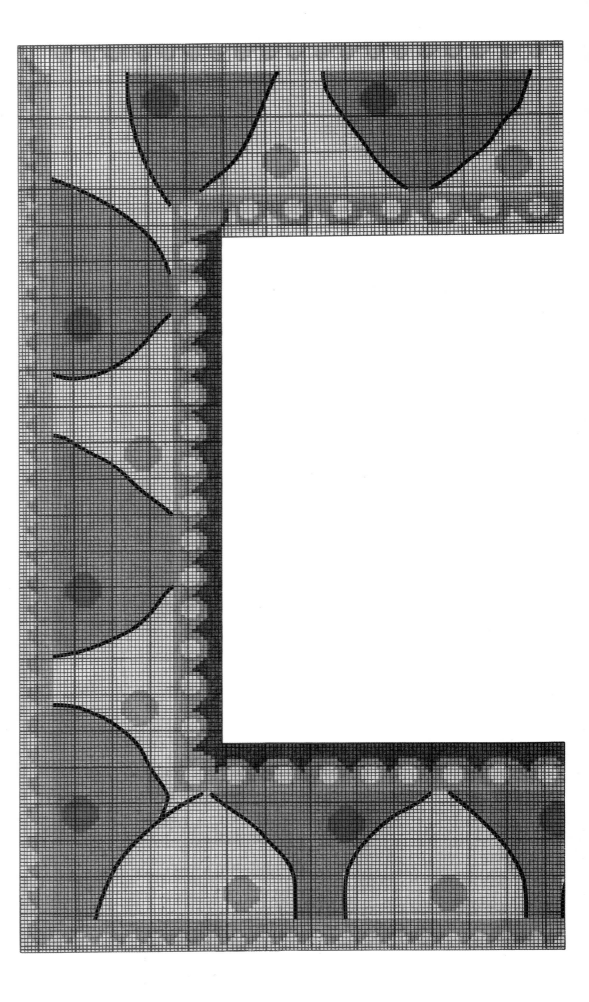

TOP

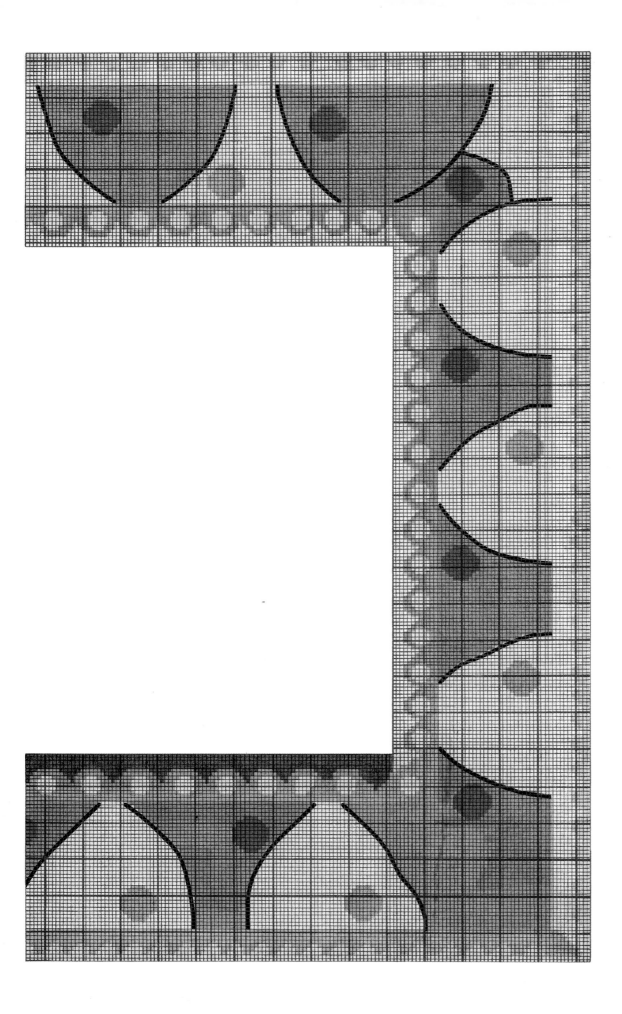

THE BLOTTER

Vanessa Bell's design for a blotter is based on a simple floral theme and worked entirely in half-cross stitch. It is displayed along with the spectacle case (see page 44), and one wonders how many wonderful letters were pressed between its covers before being dispatched to their final destination. Because the original needlepoint is quite fine, I have worked the piece using two strands of yarn. However, three strands would produce a more substantial fabric, if that is preferred.

YARNS

Pa540	1gm	(0.04oz)	■
Pa551	2gm	(0.07oz)	■
Pa583	2gm	(0.07oz)	■
Pa320	1gm	(0.04oz)	■
Pa950	2gm	(0.07oz)	■
Pa962	3gm	(0.12oz)	■
Pa493	42gm	(1.48oz)	■
Pa852	4gm	(0.14oz)	■
Pa823	2gm	(0.07oz)	■
Pa723	2gm	(0.07oz)	■
Pa725	3gm	(0.12oz)	■
Pa714	2gm	(0.07oz)	□
Pa640	2gm	(0.07oz)	■
Pa645	32gm	(1.13oz)	■
Pa603	3gm	(0.12oz)	■
PaD501	6gm	(0.21oz)	■
Ap710/4*	3gm	(0.12oz)	■
Pa462	3gm	(0.12oz)	■
Pa453	2gm	(0.07oz)	■
Pa434	1gm	(0.04oz)	■
Pa201	6gm	(0.21oz)	■

Pa = Paterna tapestry yarn.
Ap = Appleton's crewel wool.
Use two strands throughout for both, except:
* Use three strands.

MATERIALS
Tapestry yarns in the colours and quantities shown *left*.
Antique finish, 10-mesh double canvas. 43cm (17in) by 39.5cm (15½in).
Size 18 tapestry needle.
Equipment for preparing the canvas (see page 114), for blocking (see page 117) and for making up (see page 117).
Four sheets of cardboard, each 33cm (13in) by 29.2cm (11½in).
Two pieces of peach-coloured linen, each 43cm (17in) by 39.5cm (15½in).
One piece of pale blue linen, 43cm (17in) by 39.5cm (15½in).
One piece of pale blue linen, 38cm (15in) by 15cm (6in).
One 38cm (15in) length of beige cord.

WORKING THE DESIGN
Once you have prepared the canvas (see page 114), mount it on a frame (see page 115). Using two strands of yarn throughout, except where stated (see left), follow the chart on the *right* and work the entire design in half-cross stitch.

BLOCKING AND MAKING UP
Block and finish your completed needlepoint (see page 117). Once the blocked work is thoroughly dry, make it up into the blotter, using the illustrations and instructions shown on page 118 for guidance.

The design measures 33cm (13in) by 29.2cm (11½in).

DUNCAN GRANT'S BEDROOM

Duncan Grant's Bedroom, together with an adjoining Dressing Room, is on the first floor of Charleston, next to Maynard Keynes's Bedroom and above the Dining Room at the front of the house. When Vanessa Bell, Duncan Grant and 'Bunny' Garnett first moved in, in the late summer of 1916, Vanessa thought the room would make a good studio; natural light being provided by a window offering a very attractive view eastwards across the pond in front of the house. However, it soon became Duncan Grant's Bedroom and remained as such for over fifty years, apart from a brief period in December 1918 when Vanessa took over the room to give birth to her daughter Angelica.

This room was one of the first to be decorated. The existing wallpaper was initially covered with the pale-green paint also used in many of the other rooms in the house, and Vanessa Bell painted the fireplace and the two doors in sympathetic colours and motifs in 1918. Later, *c.* 1925-30, she tiled the hearth and decorated the *embrasure* of the window and a firescreen.

As far as needlepoint is concerned, this is one of the most important rooms in the house. The finest example is a bold but elegant Regency day-bed with an abstract-patterned needlepoint cover designed by Duncan Grant in 1943. A huge 'music stool' with a cross-stitch seat cover designed 1924-25 by Duncan Grant, a 19th-century chair with a needlepoint seat cover designed *c.* 1924 by Vanessa, and a 18th-century curved back chair with a needlepoint seat cover, possibly designed by Roger Fry *c.* 1925, complete the ensemble. Other furniture includes a

Various personal possessions of Duncan Grant, including a Victorian japanned cabinet, sit on the 19th-century, French provincial writing desk in his bedroom. The needlepoint chairseat cover was possibly designed by Roger Fry c. 1920-21.

Vanessa Bell decorated the fireplace in Duncan Grant's Bedroom in 1918. The picture above, a copy of Raphael's St Catherine *(c. 1922) by Vanessa, is flanked by a pair of 19th-century French apothecary's jars.*

veneered writing desk and a chest of drawers, both 19th-century French provincial, and two Irish *prie-dieu* chairs with considerable areas of beadwork. In the Dressing Room, there is a table with a magnificent painted top (c. 1945), by Duncan Grant, depicting *Arion on a dolphin.*

Of the other textiles in the two rooms, the splendid rug on the floor of the bedroom was designed by Duncan Grant in 1925 and worked in cross-stitch needlepoint by his mother, Ethel, while the curtains at the window are made from the *Urn* fabric that Duncan Grant designed c. 1943 for Allan Walton Ltd. (The curtains at the Dressing Room window are made of *Maud* fabric, which was designed in 1913 by Vanessa Bell for the Omega Workshops.) Other important items include a bust of Vanessa, a plaster cast of a Benin head on the bedroom windowsill (the original is in the British Museum) and a bedside lampstand decorated by Duncan Grant with

brightly coloured floral and leaf motifs c. 1930-35.

Among the paintings in the room are a wash drawing of *Angelica at the piano* (c. 1940) and *Nerissa in a white shirt* (c. 1965), both by Duncan Grant and of his daughter and granddaughter respectively. Paintings by Vanessa Bell include *Still life with beer bottle (1913)*, which hangs on the wall at the side of the bed, and a portrait of *Lady Strachey* (1921), Duncan Grant's aunt. However, the *Study for the frieze 'Bellum' in the Salon du Roi, Palais Bourbon*, executed in pencil by Eugene Delacroix c. 1833-34, must be considered the most significant work of art in the room. The drawing was bought by J. M. Keynes at the *Vente Degas* in Paris, 1918, and presented to Duncan Grant; Grant having informed Keynes of the sale of Degas's collection and having persuaded him to ask the British Government to fund the National Gallery's purchase of works by Ingres, Delacroix, Gauguin and Manet for the nation.

The seat cover of this large Victorian music stool was designed by Duncan Grant in 1924-5, and worked in cross-stitch needlepoint by his mother, Ethel Grant. The stool was exhibited at the Independent Gallery, London, in 1925.

The needlepoint cover of the magnificent Regency period English day-bed which stands under Duncan Grant's bedroom window was designed by Vanessa Bell c. 1930-35. Made up by Duncan's mother, Ethel, the bulk of the cover was worked in half-cross stitch, while the black lines were embroidered on top of the needlepoint in stem stitch.

The door between Duncan Grant's Bedroom and the adjoining Dressing Room was decorated by Vanessa Bell in February 1918, and painted at the same time and in the same style as the door to the main room. The three silhouette paintings that stand on top of the bookshelves are by Duncan Grant and depict relations of the family.

THE DAY-BED

A book on Bloomsbury needlepoint would not be complete without the inclusion of Duncan Grant's day-bed. Taking the bed apart proved particularly interesting. For example, while the design appears to include contrasting areas of black and brown, in fact all the brown areas were once black. This goes to show that different qualities of yarn, subjected to light, dirt and general wear and tear, fade at different rates.

Close inspection also revealed that the original design was intended to be far more elaborate than the finished piece turned out to be. The scalloped design in the middle panel was not worked in needlepoint. What you can see now are Grant's penmarks, which have gradually surfaced after many years of wear and tear and cleaning and which obviously outline his original design concept. I felt that the penmarks should be included in the project, and they have been worked on the chart in pale grey.

When including a piece of this size in a book such as this, one has to consider its practical use. If you happen to have a magnificent day-bed knocking around the house, then you are very lucky and have the opportunity to make up this wonderful design exactly as Duncan Grant intended. However, for those of us who are not so lucky, I suggest you consider working the needlepoint in sections and making it up into three separate cushions. I have not supplied weights for the yarns listed right, since they would vary according to your choice of canvas size.

 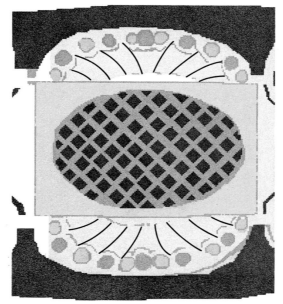 

YARNS

Ap930/4	▨
Pa864	▨
Pa486	☐
Pa443	▨
Pa444	☐
Pa445	☐
Ap473	▨
Pa203	▨
Pa465	☐
Pa220	▨

Pa = Paterna tapestry yarn.
Use two strands throughout.

Ap = Appleton's crewel wool.
Use three strands throughout.

The design for the complete day-bed measures 68.5cm (27in) by 155cm (61in).
The design for cushions one and three measures 68.5cm (27in) by 24cm (9½in).
The design for cushion two measures 68.5cm (27in) by 42cm (16½in).

MATERIALS

Tapestry yarns in the colours shown *below*.
Antique finish, 10-mesh double canvas. 79cm (31in) by 165cm (65in) for the complete piece; 79cm (31in) by 121cm (47½in) for three cushions. Size 18 tapestry needle.
Equipment for preparing the canvas (*see* page 114), for blocking (*see* page 117) and for making up (*see* page 117).

WORKING THE DESIGN

As a day-bed:
Once you have prepared the canvas (*see* page 114), mount it on a frame (*see* page 115). Using two or three strands of yarn (as specified *left*) and following the charts on the right and the following pages, work the main body of the design in half-cross stitch. Work the black lines in the middle panel by embroidering over the finished needlepoint in stem stitch.

As three separate cushions:
Prepare and mount the canvas as above. For cushion one, use two or three strands of yarn (as specified in the key) and work the first 95 rows of the chart only in half-cross stitch. Then square up the edges in white. For cushion two, use two strands of yarn throughout and work rows 96 to 260 inclusive in half-cross stitch. Work the black lines by embroidering over the needlepoint in stem stitch and, again, square up the edges in white. For cushion three, use two or three strands of yarn (as specified in the key) and work the last 95 rows of the chart (261 onward) in half-cross stitch. As before, square up the edges in white.

BLOCKING AND MAKING UP

Block and finish your completed needlepoint (*see* page 117). Once the blocked work is thoroughly dry, either make up into cushions (*see* page 117) or, if you have worked the needlepoint as a single cover for a day-bed, you should call on the services of a professional upholsterer.

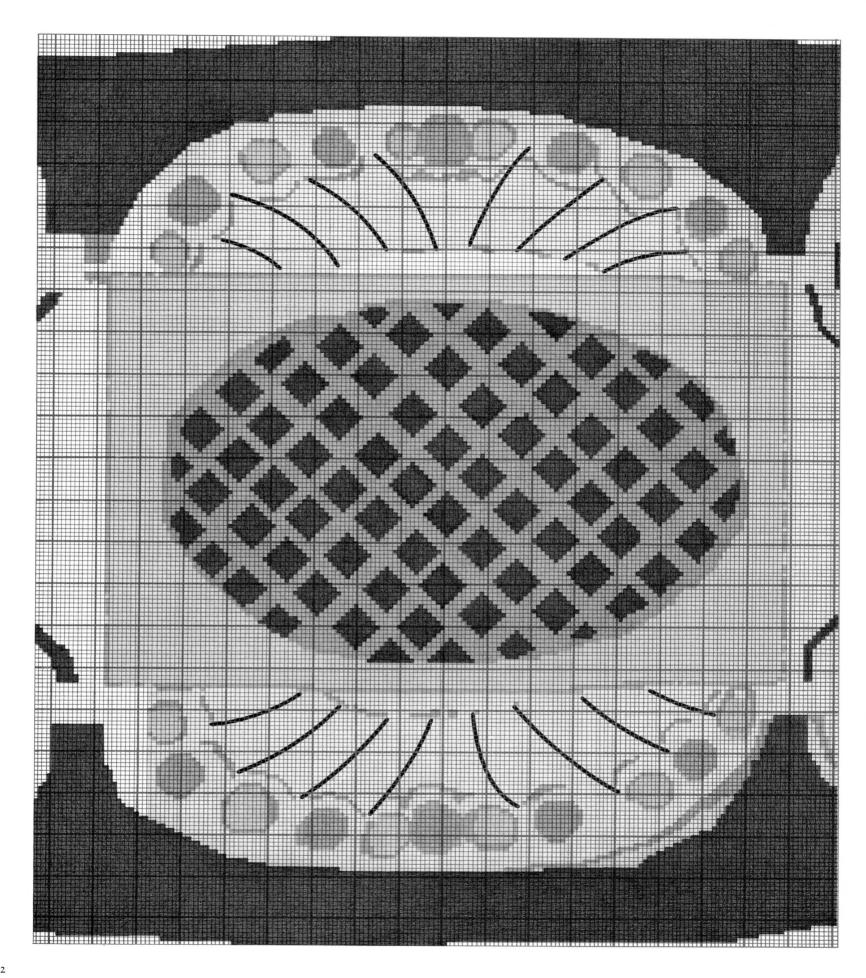

THE CHARLESTON RUG

The glorious Charleston rug was designed by Duncan Grant. It consists of two repeat patterns worked in different directions, plus a border. The original was made up in sections and then sewn together, and since the finished rug measures 162.5cm (64in) by 178cm (70in) I have split the piece into four borders and a middle panel divided into 12 blocks. Before you begin, please note the varying sizes of the blocks and the fact that if you wish to alter the size of the rug you can do so by adding or subtracting blocks and adjusting the size of the borders accordingly. Weights for the yarns have not been given because they will vary considerably according to the size you wish the rug to be.

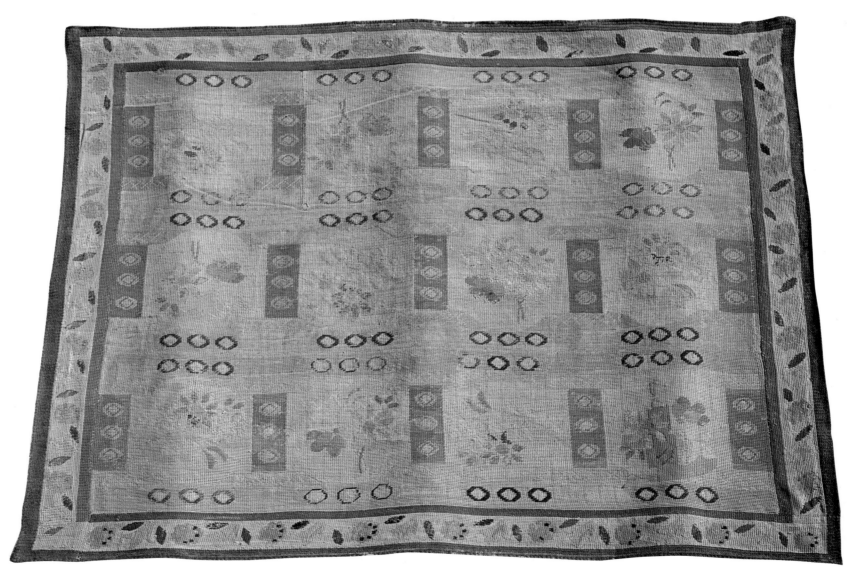

YARNS

Ap930/4	■	Ap290/3	☐
Ap710/5	■	Ap640/2	☐
Ap140/4	■	Ap330/6	☐
Ap750/3	☐	Ap240/3	☐
Ap140/1	☐	Ap340/1	☐
Ap200/9	■	Ap310/1	☐
Ap200/4	☐	Ap330/1	☐
Ap620/5	■	PaD500	■
Ap 620/5 and		PaD501	☐
		Ap740/7	■
Ap620/3	☐	Ap920/4	■
Ap620/3	☐	Ap920/1	☐
Ap690/6 and		Ap960/6	■
		Ap960/3	■
Ap180/4	☐	Ap970/6	■
Ap690/5	☐	Ap980/8	☐
Ap840/2	☐	PaD133	☐
Ap400/4	■		

Ap = Appleton's crewel wool.
Use five strands throughout, except when stated otherwise in Working the Design.

Pa = Paterna tapestry yarn.
Use four strands throughout.

The design measures:
Middle panel: 149.8cm (59in) by 143.5cm (56½in).
Top and bottom borders: 172.7cm (68in) by 15cm (6in).
Side borders: 150cm (59in) by 15cm (6in).
Assembled rug: 177.8cm (70in) by 162.5cm (64in).
Use four strands throughout.

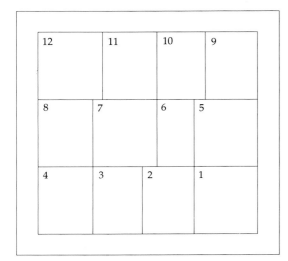

MATERIALS

Tapestry yarns in the colours shown *left*.
Antique finish, 6-mesh double canvas throughout.
The middle panel, divided into 12 blocks, measures 160cm (63in) by 153.5cm (60½in) – includes selvedge.
The borders of the rug are made up of four separate strips of canvas:
Top and bottom borders are 183cm (72in) by 25cm (10in) – includes selvedge.
Side borders are 160cm (63in) by 25cm (10in) – includes selvedge.
Size 16 tapestry needle.
Equipment for preparing the canvas (*see* page 114), for blocking (*see* page 117) and for making up (*see* page 117).

WORKING THE DESIGN

Once you have prepared the canvas (*see* page 114), mount it on a frame (*see* page 115). Using four or five strands of yarn (as specified in the key), follow the chart on the following pages and work the middle panel in half-cross stitch, sloping the stitches downward from right to left. Work the 12 blocks that make up the middle panel horizontally from right to left, as follows:

Block 1: (bottom right-hand corner, 102 by 113 holes)
Work chart 2 over the first 84 holes, then repeat the first 18 squares of the chart to complete the block.
Block 2: (84 by 113 holes)
Work chart 1, reading it upside-down (i.e. the top becomes the bottom).
Block 3: (84 by 113 holes)
Work chart 2, reading it upside-down.
Block 4: (84 by 113 holes)
Work chart 1.
Block 5: (placed directly above block 1, 102 by 113 holes)
Work the first 18 squares of chart 2, then work chart 1 upside-down.
Block 6: (66 by 113 holes)
Starting at square 19, work chart 2.
Block 7: (102 by 113 holes)
Work chart 1, then repeat the first 18 squares of chart 1.
Block 8: (84 by 113 holes)
Work chart 2 upside-down.
Block 9: (placed directly above block 5, 84 by 113 holes).
Work the first 18 squares of chart 1, then work the first 66 squares of chart 2 upside-down.

Block 10: (84 by 113 holes)
Work chart 1.
Block 11: (84 by 113 holes)
Work chart 2.
Block 12: (84 by 113 holes)
Work the first 18 squares of chart 2, then work chart 1 upside-down. Once you have completed the blocks, start working the borders following the chart below. Work the mustard-coloured area of border in half-cross stitch, sloping down from left to right. Work the flower panel on the border in half-cross stitch, sloping from right to left. Work the brown-coloured outer area of border in cross stitch . . . all as follows:
Top and bottom borders: (424 by 35 holes)
Work 45 squares of the chart 7 times, then repeat the first 39 squares.
Side borders: (339 by 35 holes)
Work 8 stitches in cross stitch in yarn Ap930/4, then work 20 squares from the chart, excluding the top stripe in yarn Ap330/6. Continue in pattern from square 21 until you have worked 8 repeats in total. Then repeat the first 21 squares again, omitting the top stripe. Finish by working 8 stitches in cross stitch with yarn Ap930/4.

BLOCKING AND MAKING UP

Block and finish your completed needlepoint (*see* page 117). Once the blocked work is thoroughly dry, turn the selvedge back on all pieces of canvas and baste flat. Then, working from the wrong side, sew the middle panel to the borders using overcast stitch and toning wool. Next, work the leaf design (*see* chart) to finish off the motifs at the corners. Finally, prepare the back of the rug for use (*see* page 117).

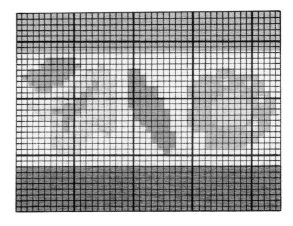

Chart 1

Chart 2

67

THE MUSIC STOOL

The music stool is one of the few pieces at Charleston that time has been kind to. It sits in a shady corner away from the sunlight and while sharper colours, unexposed to the fading effects of light and dirt, might be evident on the wrong side of the work, I decided for the purposes of this project to match the colours to those on the right side, as they had stood up so well to the passing years.

The actual stool cover, designed by Duncan Grant in 1925, has a border worked in cross stitch in a Florentine pattern, although a chart for this is not included. The stool itself measures approximately 70cm (27½in) by 84cm (33in). Since this is much larger than the average stool, you might find it more appropriate to use the design, which has been charted to the size of the original, for a rug, a wall-hanging or a large cushion. Alternatively, the piece could be reduced in size by using a canvas with less holes to the cm/in.

Since I have not re-made this design I can not give accurate weights for the yarns. However, you will not go far wrong if you purchase one skein of each colour. Also, by the time this book is published, the canvas will have been re-worked and kits containing the correct quantities of yarn will be available.

YARNS

Pa900	▣	Pa643	▢
Pa912	▢	Pa644	▢
Pa922	▣	Pa604	▣
Pa923	▣	Pa534	▢
Pa924	▢	Pa510	▣
PaD211	▣	Pa511	▢
PaD275	▢	Pa320	▣
Pa870	▣	Pa421	▣
Pa872	▣	Pa470	▣
Pa481	▣	Pa474	▢
Pa484	▢	Pa430	▣
Pa880	▣	Pa453	▣
Pa862	▢	Pa454	▢
PaD411	▢	Pa413	▢
PaD419	▣	Pa414	▢
Pa731	▢	Pa462	▣
Pa751	▢	Pa464	▢
Pa444	▢	PaD346	▣
PaD531	▢	PaD391	▢
Pa651	▣	Pa204	▢
Pa652	▣	Pa220	▓

Pa = Paterna tapestry yarn.
Use four strands throughout.

MATERIALS

Tapestry yarns in the colours and quantities shown *left*.
Antique finish, 6-mesh double canvas. 80cm (31½in) by 94cm (37in).
Size 16 tapestry needle.
Equipment for preparing the canvas (*see* page 114), for blocking (*see* page 117) and for making up (*see* page 117).

WORKING THE DESIGN

Once you have prepared the canvas (*see* page 114), mount it on a frame (*see* page 115). Using four strands of yarn throughout, follow the chart on the following page and work the entire design in cross stitch.

BLOCKING AND MAKING UP

Block and finish your completed needlepoint (*see* page 117). Once the blocked work is thoroughly dry, make it up into a stool cover or, alternatively, a rug (*see* page 117), a wall-hanging (*see* page 118) or a large cushion (*see* page 117).

The finished design measures 69.8cm (27½in) by 83.8cm (33in).

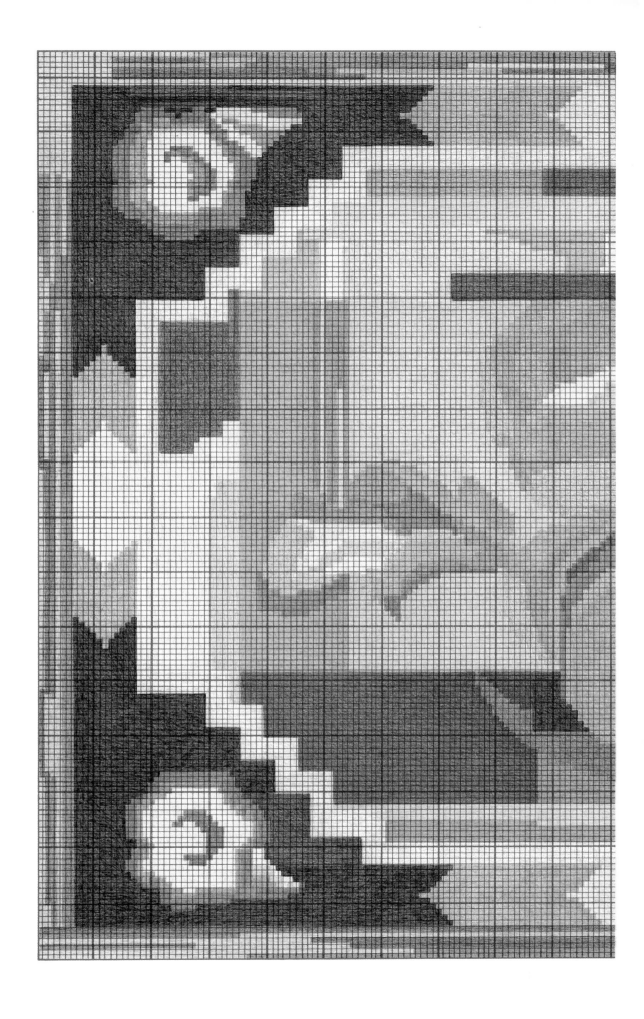

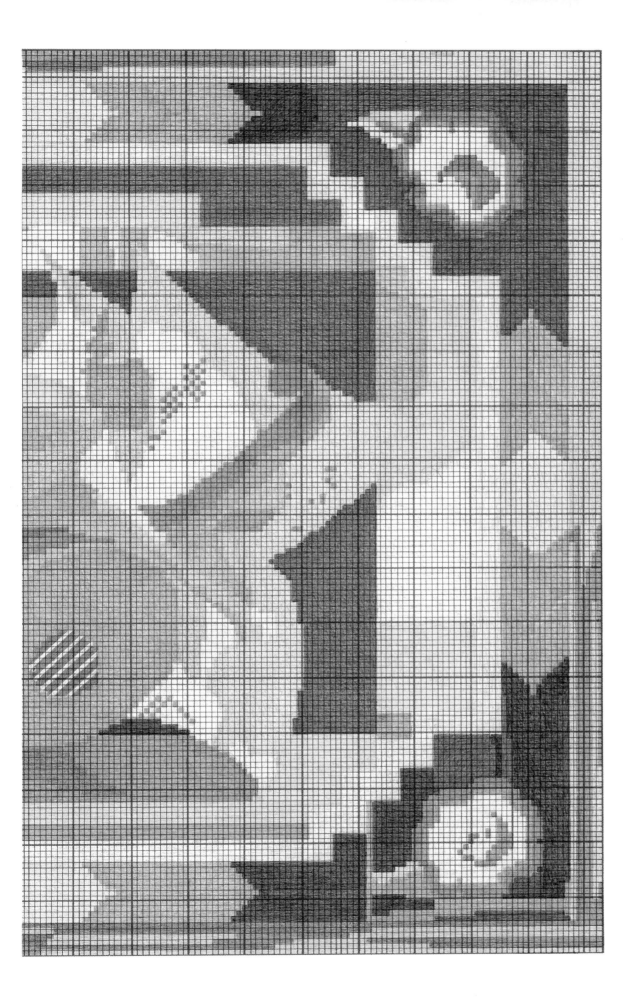

MAYNARD KEYNES'S BEDROOM

John Maynard Keynes, economist, writer, Fellow and Bursar of King's College Cambridge and an intimate friend of Duncan Grant and Vanessa Bell, was a frequent guest at Charleston between 1917-1925. The room which was set aside for him is on the first floor at the front of the house, between Duncan Grant's Bedroom and Clive Bell's Bedroom, and has a window looking out over the pond and across the fields to Tilton, where Keynes eventually made his home.

Keynes had been the chief representative of the British Treasury at the Paris Peace Conference after the First World War, but had resigned in protest over the reparations the victorious Allies were intent on imposing on Germany. 'Retiring' to Charleston, and bringing his own servants from his house in Gordon Square, London, with him, Keynes wrote his famous polemic, *The Economic Consequences of the Peace*, most of which was composed in his bedroom between June and October of 1919.

Unlike many of the other rooms in the house, Keynes's Bedroom remains unembellished by decorative features apart, that is, from a stained glass panel by Quentin Bell, *c.* 1940, which is set in the door. However, the plain walls provide a contrasting and understated backdrop to the richly decorated furniture, the most striking piece being the 'Morpheus' bedhead, originally painted *c.* 1917 by Duncan Grant for Vanessa Bell. Together with a linen chest, painted *c.* 1917, which portrays 'Leda and the duck' on the inside of the lid, and the 'Lilypond' table, designed 1913-14 for the Omega Workshops, the bedhead is one of the most notable items of decorated furniture that still survives today from Duncan Grant's early period.

Other items of furniture in the room include a late 18th-century Dutch chair (one from a set of six) with a needlepoint seat cover depicting a bowl of fruit, designed by Vanessa Bell c. 1924; a mid-19th century, rush-seated 'Sussex settle', given to the house by Mary Hutchinson (Clive Bell's lover and a patron of Duncan Grant and Vanessa Bell); two (moveable) decorative panels, used as a firescreen and painted by Duncan Grant in the 1930s, and a bookcase, painted by Quentin Bell in the 1970s and containing files of copies of correspondence between Virginia Woolf and Clive and Vanessa Bell. A terracotta bust of Quentin Bell stands on top of the bookcase.

Also in the room are various plates and pottery figures and a lampshade on a table beside the bed, all made by Quentin Bell after 1939 and decorated either by Quentin himself, his mother Vanessa or Jane Simone ('Janie') Bussy, the daughter of Lytton Strachey's elder sister Dorothy and a painter and translator who served in the French Resistance during the Second World War.

Of the ten paintings in Maynard Keynes's Bedroom, three are by Vanessa Bell: *The Duomo, Luccas* (1949); *Brighton pier* (c. 1955), and *Chattie Salaman* (c. 1940). (Salaman had a distinguished career in the theatre and was a friend of Vanessa's daughter, Angelica.) Five paintings are by Duncan Grant: *A Portrait of Adrian Stephen* (1910), the younger brother of Virginia Woolf and Vanessa Bell and a regular visitor to Charleston; *Julian Bell reading* (c. 1930); on a corner cupboard, *A Still life with Staffordshire figure and wine bottle* (c. 1940); *Helen Anrep in the dining room, Charleston* (c. 1945) (Anrep was a frequent visitor and lived with Roger Fry from 1926 until his death), and *The barns, Charleston* (1959). (Adrian Stephen was one of the perpetrators of the 'dreadnought hoax'; in which he, Virginia, Duncan and others dressed up as the Emperor of Abyssinia and his retinue and were given a tour of the flagship of the British Fleet, HMS *Dreadnought*, to the consternation of the Admiralty.) There is also a painting of *The garden* (c. 1938-40) by Elizabeth Watson, a friend of Quentin Bell and secretary of the Artists' International Association during the late 1930s.

This richly coloured stained glass panel is set in the door of the bedroom that Vanessa Bell and Duncan Grant set aside for Maynard Keynes during his regular visits to Charleston. It was designed c. 1940 by Quentin Bell, the younger son of Vanessa and Clive Bell, whose room it eventually became; and is, unusually, the only permanent decorative feature in the room.

The late 18th-century Dutch chair (one of a set of six) in Maynard Keynes's Bedroom has a half-cross stitch needlepoint seat cover designed by Vanessa Bell c. 1924.

Below: *The 'Morpheus' bedhead, in Keynes's Bedroom, was decorated by Duncan Grant for Vanessa Bell c. 1917. Vanessa's initials (VB) are painted in the form of a medallion 'hung' from a ribbon, on the back of the headboard (not shown). Morpheus, the god of sleep who sends 'dreams and visions of human form' to the sleeper, appears in Ovid's Metamorphoses II.*

Right: *Painted at Charleston c. 1917 by Duncan Grant, the linen chest is decorated inside and out, and portrays 'Leda and the duck' on the underside of the lid. Together with the 'Morpheus' bedhead and the 'Lilypond' table (not shown) the linen chest is one of three notable examples of decorated furniture from Grant's early period that stand in Keynes's room.*

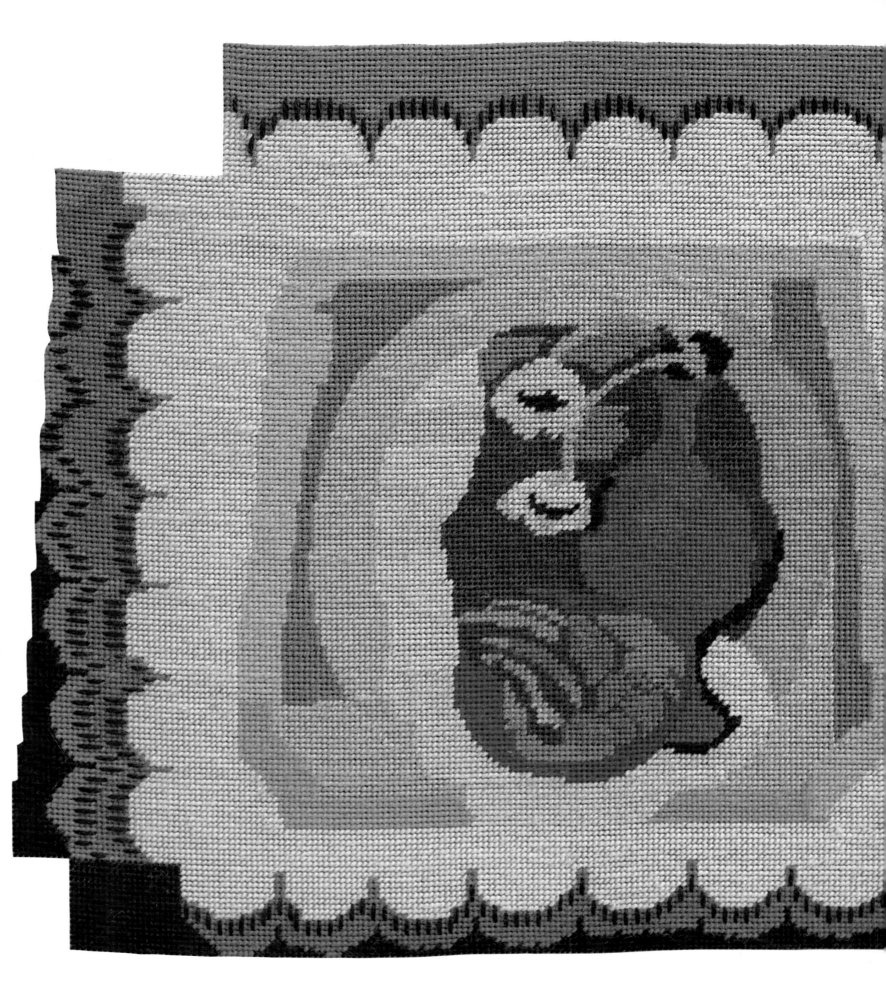

VASE OF FLOWERS CHAIRSEAT COVER

Vanessa Bell's original vase of flowers design for a chairseat has faded almost beyond recognition. However, close inspection revealed subtle variations of colour which, in combination with the simplicity of image, added greatly to the appeal of the piece. The original needlepoint was worked in cross stitch, but I have reproduced it in half-cross stitch in order to speed up the time it takes to complete the project. I would suggest that the design could be squared up and worked as a cushion cover or a wall-hanging, as an alternative to a covering for a chairseat.

MATERIALS

Tapestry yarns in the colours and quantities shown *right*.
Antique finish, 10-mesh double canvas. 62cm (24½in) by 53cm (21in).
Size 18 tapestry needle.
Equipment for preparing the canvas (*see* page 114), for blocking (*see* page 117) and for making up (*see* page 117).

WORKING THE DESIGN

Once you have prepared the canvas (*see* page 114), mount it on a frame (*see* page 115). Using two or three strands throughout (as specified *right*), follow the chart on the following page and work the entire design in half-cross stitch.

BLOCKING AND MAKING UP

Block and finish your completed needlepoint (*see* page 117). Once the blocked work is thoroughly dry, cover your chairseat with it. Alternatively, make it up into a cushion (*see* page 117) or a wall-hanging (*see* page 118).

The design measures (at widest point) 43.2cm (17in) by 52cm (20½in).

YARNS

Pa871	12gm	(0.42oz)	
Pa483	4gm	(0.14oz)	
Pa486	2gm	(0.07oz)	
Pa886	70gm	(2.47oz)	
Pa731	4gm	(0.14oz)	
Pa444	12gm	(0.42oz)	
Pa743	4gm	(0.14oz)	
Ap840/3	5gm	(0.18oz)	
Ap840/2	5gm	(0.18oz)	
Pa421	6gm	(0.21oz)	
Pa450	18gm	(0.63oz)	
Pa411	4gm	(0.14oz)	
Pa413	5gm	(0.18oz)	
Ap930/1	15gm	(0.53oz)	
Pa464	8gm	(0.28oz)	
Ap330/5	3gm	(0.12oz)	
Pa652	3gm	(0.12oz)	
Pa603	2gm	(0.07oz)	
Ap540/1	3gm	(0.12oz)	
Pa663	6gm	(0.21oz)	
Pa664	18gm	(0.63oz)	
Ap560/6	10gm	(0.35oz)	
Ap320/1	20gm	(0.70oz)	
Pa220	10gm	(0.35oz)	
Ap960/6	5gm	(0.18oz)	
Pa200	3gm	(0.12oz)	
Pa202	6gm	(0.21oz)	

Pa = Paterna tapestry yarn.
Use two strands throughout.

Ap = Appleton's crewel wool.
Use three strands throughout.

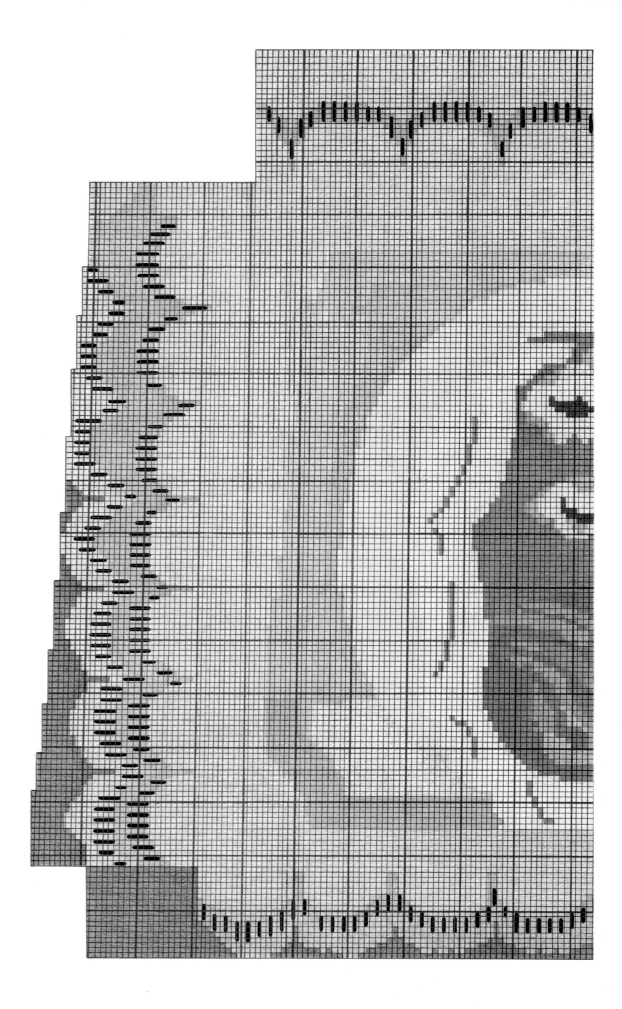

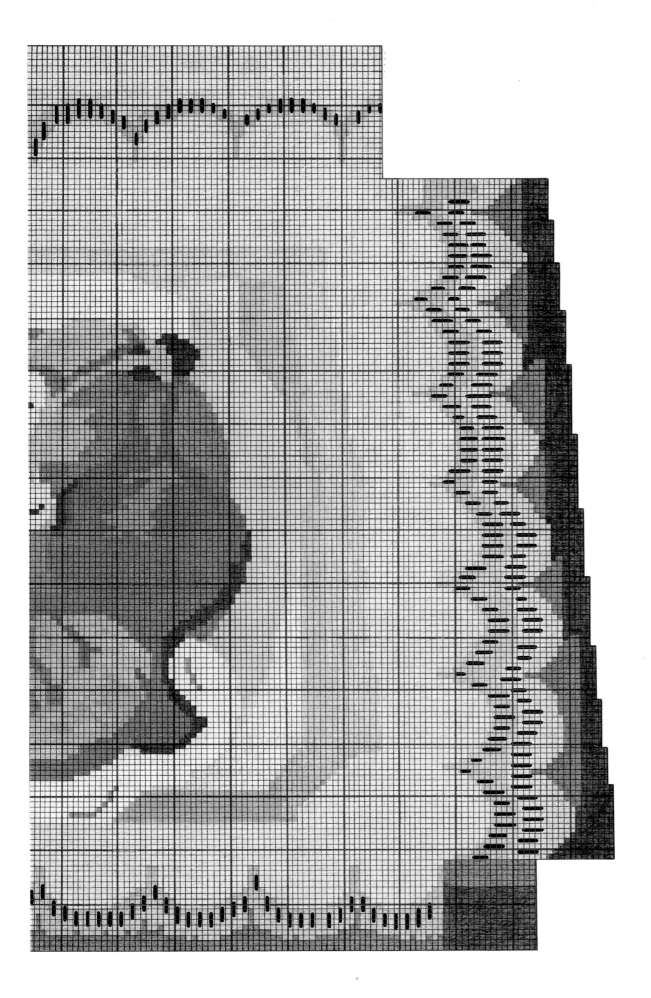

BOWL OF FRUIT CHAIRSEAT COVER

Abstract images of fruit and flowers are familiar themes at Charleston, and this chairseat cover complements several of the painted occasional tables and cupboard panels throughout the house. Worked in half-cross stitch, the design can be adapted for a modern chair or squared up to form a cushion or wall-hanging.

MATERIALS
Tapestry yarns in the colours and quantities shown *right*.
Antique finish, 10-mesh double canvas. 65cm (25½in) by 55cm (21½in).
Equipment for preparing the canvas (*see* page 114), for blocking (*see* page 117) and for making up (*see* page 117).

WORKING THE DESIGN
Once you have prepared the canvas (*see* page 114), mount it on a frame (*see* page 115). Using two or three strands of yarn throughout (as specified *right*) and following the chart on the following page, work the entire design in half-cross stitch.

BLOCKING AND MAKING UP
Block and finish your completed needlepoint (*see* page 117). Once the blocked work is thoroughly dry, you can make it up into a chairseat cover (*see* page 117) or a wall-hanging (*see* page 118).

The design measures 54.6cm (21½in), at the widest point, by 44.5cm (17½in).

YARNS

Pa741	12gm	(0.42oz)	
Pa712	48gm	(1.70oz)	
Ap550/1	2gm	(0.07oz)	
Pa801	5gm	(0.18oz)	
Pa870	3gm	(0.12oz)	
Pa483	2gm	(0.07oz)	
Pa484	2gm	(0.07oz)	
Pa485	2gm	(0.07oz)	
Pa470	3gm	(0.12oz)	
PaD143	4gm	(0.14oz)	
Pa454	2gm	(0.07oz)	
Ap950/1	3gm	(0.12oz)	
PaD521	4gm	(0.14oz)	
Pa645	5gm	(0.18oz)	
Pa602	6gm	(0.21oz)	
Pa604	2gm	(0.07oz)	
PaD546	3gm	(0.12oz)	
Pa524	3gm	(0.12oz)	
Pa513	3gm	(0.12oz)	
Ap740/8	15gm	(0.53oz)	
Pa321	3gm	(0.12oz)	
Ap710/4	3gm	(0.12oz)	
Ap600/3	2gm	(0.07oz)	

Pa = Paterna tapestry yarn.
Use two strands throughout.

Ap = Appleton's crewel wool.
Use three strands throughout.

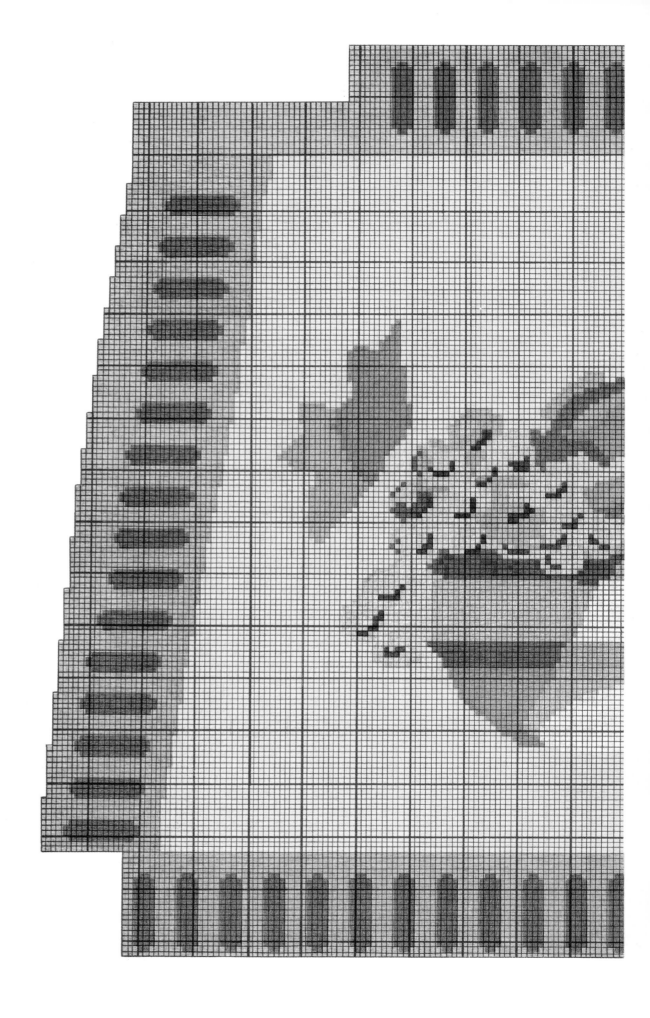

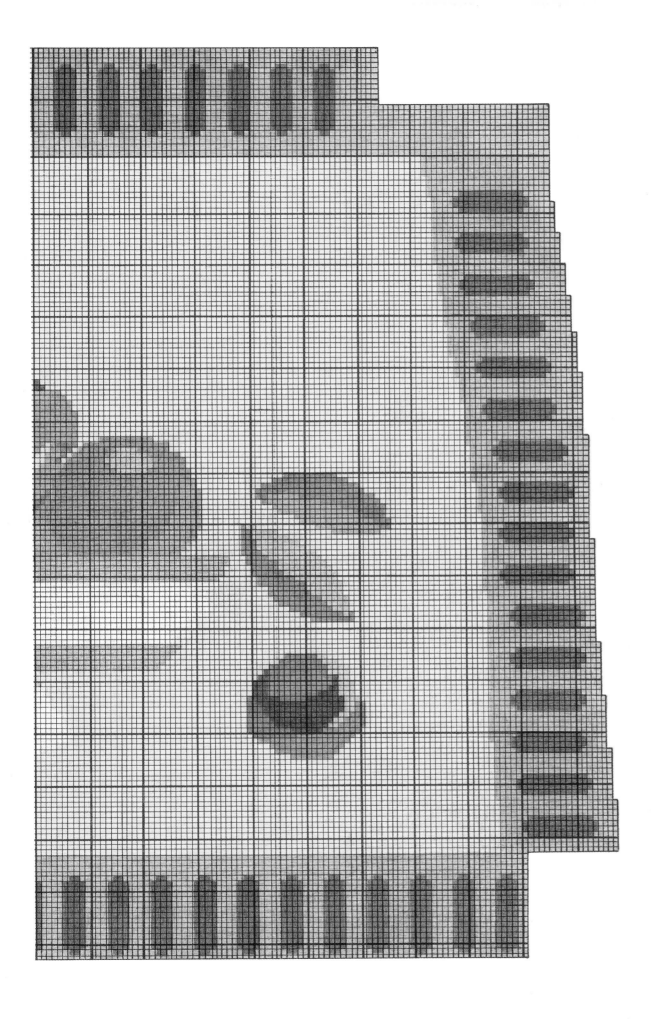

AROUND CHARLESTON

Looking back on the first few years at Charleston with Vanessa Bell and Duncan Grant, 'Bunny' Garnett wrote in *The Flowers of the Forest* (1955): 'One after another the rooms were decorated and altered almost out of recognition as the bodies of the saved are said to be glorified after the resurrection'. This campaign of creativity within the house, in which it gradually assumed a style of decoration and character that closely reflected the lifestyle and interests of its occupants, also extended to the gardens outside.

When Vanessa and her family first took out a lease in 1916, the orchard and paddock had been neglected for some years, the pond was partly overrun with weeds and the walled garden was, for the most part, given over to fruit trees and vegetables, in particular cabbages. However, as Vanessa and Duncan became increasingly enthusiastic about gardening a transformation began. In the years leading up to the Second World War much was done: flowerbeds were re-dug and filled with a profusion of brightly coloured plants and flowers; plans were drawn up for paths and a gravel terrace; various statues were introduced; a mosaic was put down, and a lawn was made with a tile-edged pool at one end of it. While the painters did much of the work, guests also helped out – Maynard Keynes, for example, regularly weeded the paths with a penknife during the early years.

The most intense period of cultivation began after Vanessa Bell became fully resident at the house once more in 1939, and under her close supervision a profusion of flowers, shrubs and vegetables were planted. Indeed,

so much was introduced that maintenance became something of a problem; a situation largely remedied by the appointment of a local pensioner, 'young Mr Stevens', as a permanent gardener.

As much as the cultivation of the garden over the years reflected the interests and energies of the occupants of the house, so it provided a constant source of inspiration for their painting. Indeed, in a letter in 1921 to Roger Fry, who was often consulted about ideas for the garden, Vanessa declared she felt rarely content to paint 'anything I don't find at my door'. Looked at retrospectively, her paintings of the garden provide a visual record of the

progress made, notably the changing aspects of the pools, the growth of trees and climbing plants on the walls, the gradual re-stocking of herbaceous borders and the sudden changes of colour resulting from Vanessa and Duncan's changed preferences each year.

Although Vanessa was undoubtedly the presiding spirit of the garden, Duncan's contributions should not be underestimated. His letters to his mother, and to Vanessa, regularly mentioned seed catalogues, planting and visits to nurseries, and he was responsible for a number of projects, including the planning of a small enclosed space, containing a pool, vines and figs, outside his Studio and

Far left: *A view from the house of some of the paths and beds in the walled garden. Reconstructed between 1984-66 under the guidance of Sir Peter Shepheard, the garden today looks as it might have appeared during the 1950s.*

Top left: *The remains of a frost-damaged female torso traditionally provided a rather unusual base for a hydrangea overlooking the mosaic Piazza. The garden was restocked by Clifton Nurseries during the mid-1980s.*

Left: *Ceramic tiles, copied by Quentin Bell from the originals hand-painted (c. 1930) by his mother, Vanessa, edge the pond in the lawn of the walled garden.*

Right: *A ciment fondu Female figure (1954), by Quentin Bell, floats above the reeds on the far bank of the large pond in front of the house.*

known as Grant's Folly. Although during the early years at Charleston Duncan had preferred to paint near the pond at the front of the house and in the cowsheds and the countryside beyond, in later years he was increasingly drawn to the walled garden as a source of inspiration.

Any description of Charleston and its occupants, gardens and interior decorations would be incomplete without a mention of the art and literary critic, Clive Bell and his contribution to life there. Married to Vanessa in 1907, and father of her two sons, Julian and Quentin, Clive maintained a separate establishment at 50 Gordon Square, London, until 1939, but stayed frequently at Charleston with Vanessa and Duncan during the inter-war years, before moving permanently to the house at the outbreak of the Second World War. He brought with him a collection of Post-Impressionist paintings that greatly enriched the interior of the house. Among them were works by Picasso, Gris and Vlaminck, gifts from French

The armchair in the Library is covered in a Laura Ashley reproduction of the Clouds *fabric designed in 1932 by Duncan Grant for Allan Walton Ltd.*

A ceramic vase, by Quentin Bell, sits on a tiled table top, designed, c. 1930 by Duncan Grant, in Clive Bell's Study on the ground floor at the front of the house.

friends such as Segonzac and Derain, and paintings and drawings by Delacroix, Modigliani, Sickert and Watts.

Almost as important as the paintings were his books. Vanessa's original bedroom on the first floor of the house was converted into a library to accommodate Clive's large collection of English, French and Classical literature. It contained early editions of Voltaire, Gibbon, Walpole, Pepys and Byron, together with numerous paperbacks of French history and fiction; the latter including works by Sartre, Camus and Colette. Clive also brought with him a large collection of art books and exhibition catalogues, most of which were kept in his study on the ground floor, and throughout his years at the house, like Vanessa and Duncan, he kept up a voluminous correspondence with numerous friends and acquantainces that kept Charleston and its occupants at the heart of current thinking in the realms of art and literature.

The fireplace in Clive Bell's Study was decorated by Vanessa Bell c. 1925-30. She wrote to her sister Virginia that sometimes the only way of staying warm was to stand in front of the fire and paint the fireplace.

THE LADY WITH A LUTE

During my first visit to Charleston I walked around the house listing all the images I wanted to include in the book as needlepoint designs. Top of my list were two cupboard panels (1925) and a log box (1916-17) by artist Duncan Grant. However, the team at Charleston were concerned that it would be extremely difficult to take these painted images and transfer them successfully to canvas, since the brushstrokes contained so many subtle shades of colouring.

Well, it is possible to reproduce the paintings as needlepoints, but, as I discovered after painting my rough of the Lady with a Lute on 10-mesh canvas, the only way to achieve the desired effect is to work the design in petit point. As I always intended to avoid projects that would take forever, I simply present, for your interest and inspiration, my partly worked canvas, which might be finished around my ninetieth birthday . . . if I live that long!

FIRESCREEN

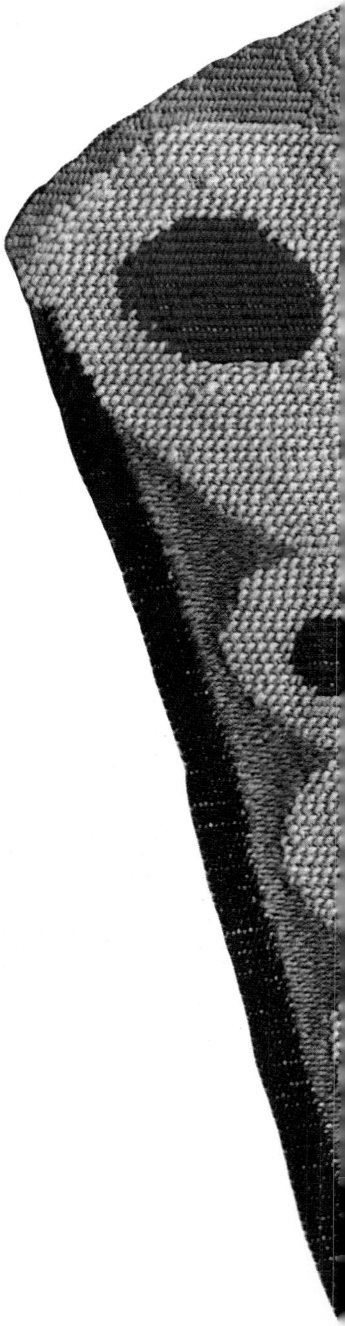

Designed by Duncan Grant, the firescreen stands in
Vanessa Bell's studio, where it is preserved in tissue;
the colours have weathered well, but the hessian
backing is now extremely frail. The circular motif used
in many of the Bloomsbury needlepoints appears here
in direct contrast to the sharp geometrics of the screen's
middle panel.

As in the Abstract-patterned cushion, which resides
in the garden room (see page 24), oblique slav stitch
has been used to create texture in the needlepoint and
each stitch is a combination of at least two colours.
Given the number of colours used, and the fact that
each stitch has been shaded, I would suggest that the
unique characteristics of the design emerged during the
sewing process, and thus cannot be precisely
reproduced. However, the firescreen does serve as an
inspiration to ways of mixing and matching needlepoint
yarns, just as one would paints and glazes, to produce
subtle and sophisticated effects.

94

SEASCAPE

This beautiful seascape, featuring a giant shell and sailing boats, is preserved in tissue paper and tucked away in Vanessa Bell's studio. Happily the colours have retained their original glory. Sewn on rough hessian, nearly every stitch is a combination of at least two and sometimes three contrasting colours, thereby creating the wonderful shaded effect. The direction of the stitches also changes frequently to highlight the edge of an image or indicate a shadow. All of this makes for a wonderful piece of needlepoint, which I would imagine was designed mostly during the sewing process. However, while I would have loved to have reproduced the seascape for you, the oversimplification required to provide a chart and accompanying instructions would have destroyed the charm of the original. Some things are best left alone to be enjoyed for what they are; in this case, a unique piece of work.

CAT ON A CABBAGE

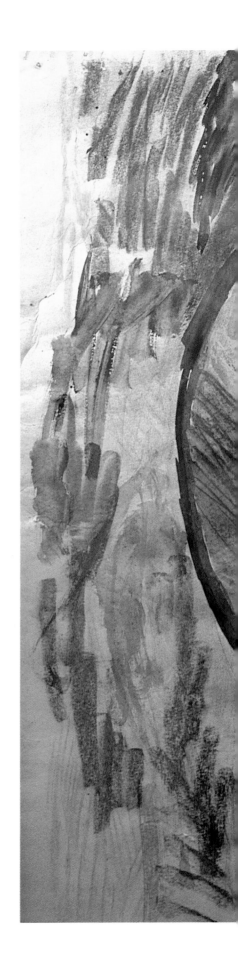

The watercolour of the original design for 'Cat on a cabbage' hangs in the studio at Charleston and is the last piece of work that visitors to the farmhouse see. It is a fascinating image since, although it is figuratively based, on first sight it appears to be simply an arrangement of blocks of colour. I assume that this design was drawn from life as the composition and positioning of the blocks suggests that the image of a cat chasing butterflies in a cabbage bed was captured by Grant at great speed before the cat decided to move on to other games.

OMEGA

The Omega Workshops were established in 1913 by Roger Fry, the art critic and painter who had organised the highly controversial Post-Impressionist Exhibitions in London, in 1910 and 1912, in which the works of Picasso, Gaugin, Matisse, Van Gogh and others were presented for the first time, to the outrage of the art establishment. Based at 33 Fitzroy Square, London, and with Vanessa Bell and Duncan Grant acting as co-directors, the Omega co-operative set out to raise what the founders considered to be the low level of artistic quality in household furnishings in England and to reflect avant-garde developments in art on the Continent by applying the ideas of the Post-Impressionists to the decoration of rooms, furniture, textiles, ceramics and murals.

During its existence (1913-19) many young avant-garde painters of the period were encouraged to come to the Workshops and design or make and paint pieces of furniture and ceramics, and paint or hand-print the bold and colourful fabrics for which the workshop quickly gained a reputation. For this they were paid ten shillings a day (a generous sum at the time). Among those who came were the sculptor Henri Gaudier-Brzeska; French painter Henri Doucet; artists Wyndham Lewis and Frederick Etchells, and 'Jessie' Etchells, who had exhibited at the Second Post-Impressionist Exhibition of 1912; the painter, writer and bohemian, Nina Hamnett; Michel Larionov, a Russian painter and theatre designer who, with his wife Nathalie Goncharova, was closely associated with Diaghilev's *Ballets Russes* and who exhibited theatre designs at the Workshops in 1919; and the painter Edward Wolfe, who had studied at the Slade school of art in London.

Many of the creations of the Workshop were undoubtedly highly innovative in terms of colour and style. However, the standard of workmanship left much to be desired, though this lack of technical prowess was, in Roger Fry's words, based on a reaction against mass-production: 'Our artists refuse to spoil the expressive quality of their work by sandpapering it down to a shop-finish, in the belief that the public has at last seen through the humbug of the machine-made imitations of works of art.'

Despite this telling criticism, there is no doubt that the Omega Workshops made an enormous contribution to contemporary thinking on interior decoration, particularly with their radical approach to the relationship between fine and applied arts. Derek Patmore, in his *Colour Schemes and Modern Furnishing* (1945), summed it up as 'a striking example of how modern artists are willing to co-operate with the interior decorator'.

As we have seen, many of the rooms at Charleston decorated by Vanessa Bell and Duncan Grant reflect the

Behind the Omega chairs in the Dining Room is a small table for the telephone, decorated with a Harlequin design, next to chintz curtains typical of the house.

Omega approach to decoration and design. They also contain several surviving pieces made at or for the Workshops. Mentioned in other chapters are the Lilypond table in Keynes' room, and the *White* and *Maud* fabrics by Vanessa Bell. Other notable examples include: six red lacquer and cane chairs designed by Roger Fry, which stand in the Dining room, and a *Still life with Omega cat*, in The Spare Bedroom, inscribed 'my first studies, Edward Wolfe. Painted 1918 in Nina Hamnett's studio Fitzroy St.' (This picture includes an Omega jug and book, and a

ceramic cat by Henri Gaudier-Brzeska sold at the Workshops.) In The Studio there is a ceramic 'Madonna and Child' made by Vanessa Bell for Omega and *Cat on a cabbage* (1913), a design in gouache by Duncan Grant for a needlepoint chair-seat sold at the Workshops. Originally in the Studio (but now in Vanessa Bell's bedroom) was the most impressive item of all: a decorative four-panel screen of largely abstract design painted by Duncan Grant for exhibition at the opening of the Workshops in July 1913.

Plates such as these on the Dining Room mantelpiece were brought back from foreign travels and reflect the untutored power of peasant art.

Left: *A print of Paul Cézanne's* Landscape in Provence *is pinned to the main door to* The Studio; *a plaster cast of the ears of Michelangelo's* David *hangs to the right of the lightswitch.*

Below: *An original plaster bust of* Virginia Woolf *(1931) by the sculptor Stephen Tomlin, husband of Julia Strachey and an occasional visitor to the house, sits on a late 18th-century Italian chest of drawers in* The Studio. *The chest was purchased in Rome in 1920 and installed here in 1939.*

A decorative panel, designed c. 1924-6 by Duncan Grant and worked in cross-stitch needlepoint by his mother Ethel, sits above open bookshelves to the left of the fireplace in The Studio. *Vanessa Bell in red kerchief, painted c. 1917 by Duncan Grant, hangs on the wall to the right. Below this is* The opera box, *painted by Jessie Etchells c. 1912. Jessie, the sister of Frederick Etchells – an associate of Roger Fry and Duncan Grant – exhibited at the Second Post-Impressionist Exhibition, in 1912, and worked for a brief period at the Omega workshops in 1913.*

VANESSA BELL'S RUG

This bold abstract design was produced by Vanessa Bell in 1913-14. She may well have designed it for a table-top, but only the painting, at the Courtauld Institute in London, has survived. The remarkable choice of colours must make it one of Vanessa Bell's finest works, and as such I felt it should be recreated as a rug and included in this collection. You should note that I found the best approach was to work the design in two halves, in cross stitch throughout, which were then joined together upon completion. I also believe that this piece would look wonderful either divided in two and mounted on a screen, or backed to make a gigantic cushion.

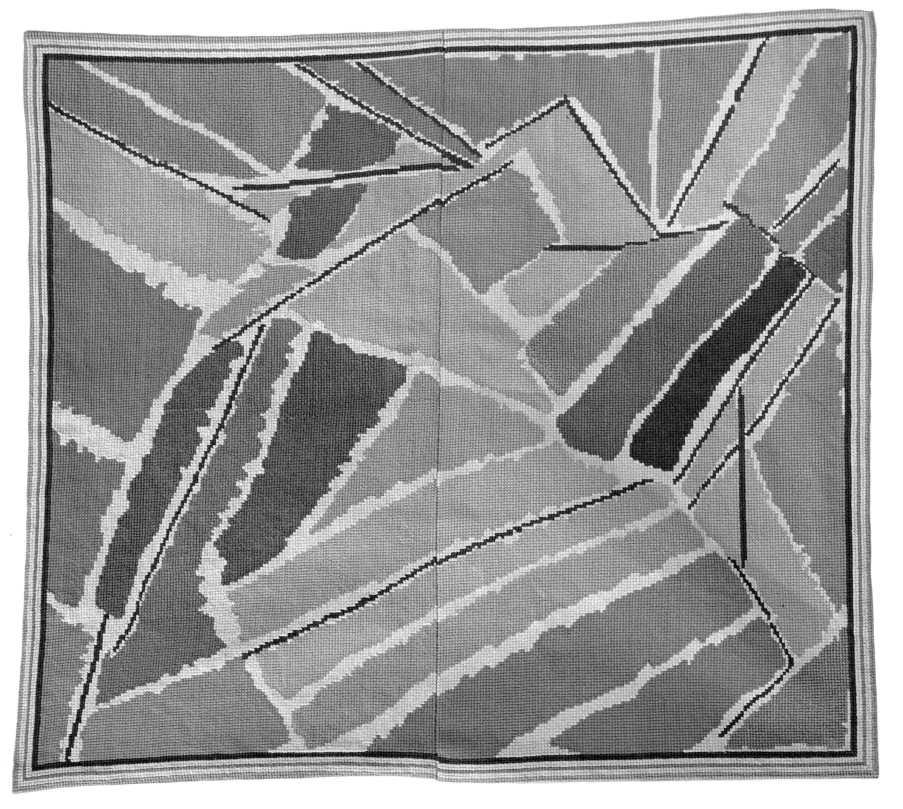

PEACOCK

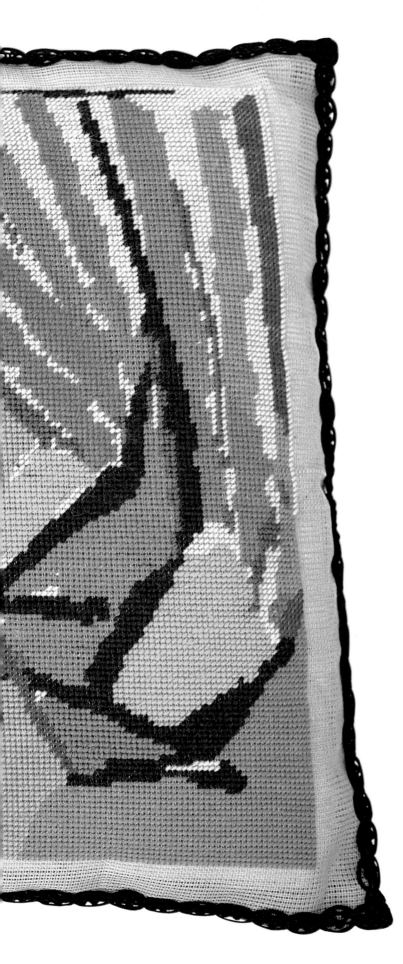

Roger Fry's peacock design was produced in 1913-14. The original painting resides at the Courtauld Institute in London; a hand-painted chiffon stole incorporating the design can also be seen in London's Victoria and Albert Museum. Boasting a glorious combination of colours, the finished needlepoint would be particularly effective made up as a cushion cover or framed as a picture.

YARNS

Ap240/2	4gm	(0.14oz)	☐
Ap240/1	4gm	(0.14oz)	☐
Pa341	7gm	(0.25oz)	■
Pa342	6gm	(0.21oz)	■
Pa312	12gm	(0.42oz)	■
Ap710/2	4gm	(0.14oz)	☐
Ap200/7	4gm	(0.14oz)	■
Ap200/6	4gm	(0.14oz)	☐
Ap200/5	4gm	(0.14oz)	☐
Ap690/4	4gm	(0.14oz)	☐
Pa221	18gm	(0.63oz)	■
Pa200	6gm	(0.21oz)	■
Pa201	5gm	(0.18oz)	■
Ap980/8	5gm	(0.18oz)	☐

Pa = Paterna tapestry yarn.
Use two strands throughout.
Ap = Appleton's crewel wool.
Use three strands throughout.

MATERIALS

Tapestry yarns in the colours and quantities shown *left*.
Antique finish, 10-mesh double canvas.
66cm (26in) by 48cm (19in).
Size 18 tapestry needle.
Equipment for preparing the canvas (*see* page 114), for blocking (*see* page 117) and for making up (*see* page 117).

WORKING THE DESIGN

Once you have prepared the canvas (*see* page 114), mount it on a frame (*see* page 115).
Using two or three strands of yarn throughout (as specified *left*), follow the chart on the following page and work the entire design in half-cross stitch. If you would prefer to work the design in cross stitch, double up the weights of the yarns given in the key.

BLOCKING AND MAKING UP

Block and finish your completed needlepoint (*see* page 117). Once the blocked work is thoroughly dry, make it up into a cushion (*see* page 117) or frame it and hang it on the wall.

The design measures 55.9cm (22in) by 38.1cm (15in).

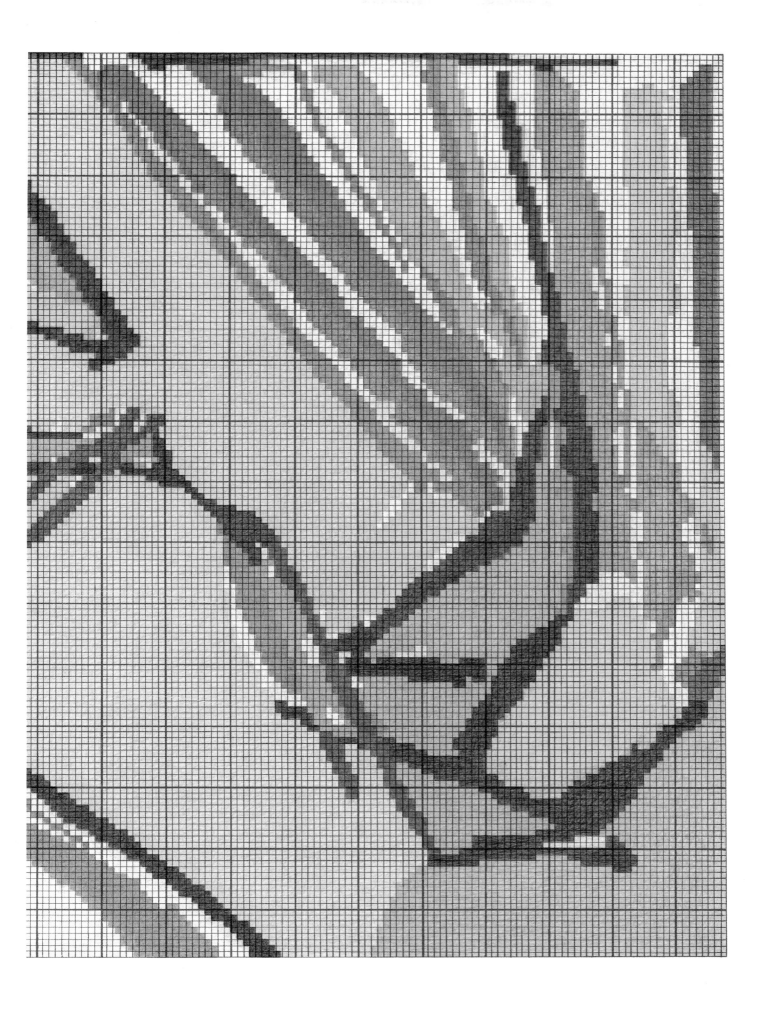

DESIGN WITH TWO FISH

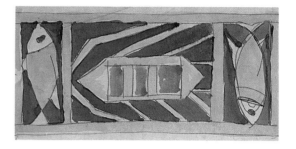

The original painting of this design, like many of the others, is in the Courtauld Institute, London. It was produced by Duncan Grant in 1913-14, and while no example of the completed work is evident, it was most certainly designed to be made up as a rug or a carpet. I felt it was particularly important to include this piece in the book as it is typical of the bold graphic designs that were produced during the Omega years and contrasts sharply with the mood of the needlepoints at Charleston.

When working from the original paintings it is difficult to assess whether the artist had completed the design or intended to modify it in some way. So, since pencil sketch marks are clearly evident on the painting, I have interpreted them in stem stitch over the finished work. I would suggest that, made up, the Design with Two Fish would be the perfect bathroom rug, or could look equally impressive as a wall-hanging.

MATERIALS AND TECHNIQUES

It was a great relief to me to discover that the stitchers of the Bloomsbury Needlepoints were far more concerned with the artistic appeal of their finished work than with the methods used to achieve it. In many cases, half stitches have been introduced to form curved edges and different weights of yarns have been used in the same needlepoint, probably more through lack of available yarns than for design reasons. Stitch types are also used in a random fashion and this approach adds to the charm and uniqueness of the finished pieces.

CANVAS

Needlepoint canvas is produced in various mesh sizes with specific numbers of holes or threads per 2.5cm (1in). For the purposes of this book, I have referred to mesh sizes as the number of holes to 2.5cm (1in), and not the number of threads. Mesh sizes can vary from as many as 32 holes per 2.5cm (1in) for extremely fine work, such as *petit point*, to as few as 3 holes per 2.5cm (1in), which is used mainly for rugmaking. In some cases *petit point* is used in the same design as half-cross stitch. When this is the case I have used double thread canvas and worked into every hole instead of every other hole.

The majority of the original designs were produced on hessian or sacking, so I have stipulated 'antique finish' canvas – which is a similar colour to sacking – in case there is any show through of canvas.

I have worked the needlepoints on a middle range of meshes, ranging from 6 – 12 holes per 2.5cm (1in), with the majority of projects worked on 10 hole, or as it is more commonly known, 10-mesh, canvas which can be covered quickly. In some instances it has been impossible to find the size mesh required to produce the exact measurements of the original work, but I have got as close as I possibly can.

There are two main types of canvas which are readily available. Single canvas, which is composed of a mesh of single interlocked threads, and double canvas, composed of double interlocked threads. With the exception of the Mirror Frame, all the designs in this book have been worked on double canvas. If you choose to use single canvas, which I wouldn't really recommend, you may have to add an extra strand of yarn to achieve good coverage. Also, you should only use the single interlocked type.

You should note that when determining the amount of canvas you require, always add at least 5cm (2in) selvedge around each edge. Canvas sizes quoted in individual projects include selvedge.

YARNS

Close colour matching has been my major priority during the completion of these projects. When working with pieces that are significant artworks, it is essential that the correct colours are adhered to since a shade off here and there can throw the whole balance of the design. I have chosen Paterna wools because I consider the quality and range of colours to be superb. Where the Paterna range could not satisfy a specific need I have used Appleton's crewel wool.

Both of these makes of yarn come in fine strands which can be doubled or trebled as required. Because the number of strands needed varies from make to make, I have quoted required quantities in gms and ozs as opposed to cms and ins. To help you in the buying process, remember that Paterna tapestry wools are sold in both 7.31mtrs (8yd) skeins and 113.5gm (4oz) hanks. A 7.31mtrs (8yd) skein contains 6gms (0.21oz) of wool and a 113.5gm (4oz) hank measures 155.5mtrs (170yds).

Paterna yarns and Appleton wools are readily available but the company addresses are also listed in our stockists' details in case you have any difficulty obtaining them. All the designs in this book are also available as mail-order kits, containing the correct amount of canvas and yarns for each project (*see* Yarn and Kit Information, page 120).

YARN QUANTITIES

The yarn quantities specified in individual projects in this book are only approximate. Do remember to increase the amount of main colour you need when altering the size of the project as described in Working the Design.

FRAMES

Many books will tell you that you have a choice as to whether or not you produce your needlepoint on a frame. Having tried both methods, I can only tell you that the work I have produced on a frame has, in some instances, not even required blocking. If you are an incredibly even stitcher then you could work a canvas on your lap. If, however, you are prone to bouts of loose or tight stitchery, do yourself a very great favour and purchase a frame before you begin.

There are various types of frames available. For most projects the straight-sided scroll frame is the most suitable. It consists of two pieces of dowling with attached webbing, on to which you sew two ends of your canvas. These pieces of dowling then slot into two uprights, which hold them rigid. You then roll the canvas on to the dowling until the fabric is absolutely taut and cleverly secure the whole thing with the four wing nuts that are supplied with the frame. Frames come in a variety of widths and should be chosen to match your work. They are very reasonably priced and well worth the money.

Another type of frame is round and consists of two circles of wood with a screw across the top. You place one circle underneath your work and clamp the second section over your work, tightening the screw until your fabric is taut. These frames come in a large range of sizes and are useful when working small needlepoints.

There are various stands available to support the frame. Some are made of beautiful polished wood, to enhance your living room, and some are stainless steel, with the emphasis on adjustability to enhance your comfort. There is a wonderful stand called an Emu, which is based on the same principle as the anglepoise lamp. Once a frame is attached it will bend and twist into so many positions that you can produce your needlepoint lying flat on your back if you so wish. It is a little ugly to live with, and can make some very strange noises as you turn and twist it, but I consider mine to be a rather eccentric pet which lives quite happily behind the sofa and enables me to sew stretched out on the couch (see Yarn and Kit Information, page 120).

NEEDLES

Tapestry needles are blunt-ended and large-eyed and come in a range of sizes beginning at 13, for heavy work, and going up to 26 for very fine work. The important thing is that the needle should take the thickness of yarn easily, and fit through the hole on the canvas without pulling it out of shape. Specific needle sizes are given for each design, but the following will serve as a useful guide.

For 18-mesh canvas use size 22 needle.
For 13- and 14-mesh canvas use size 20 needle.
For 10- and 12-mesh canvas use size 18 needle.
For 6-, 7- and 8-mesh canvas use size 16 needle.

STITCHES

HALF-CROSS STITCH

The majority of designs in this collection were produced in half-cross stitch. The diagram below shows how the stitch is worked and the end result, which is a flat slanted stitch over one row. Working the row from left to right, bring the needle up through the back of the canvas (1). Then insert it in the hole one row up and one stitch along, ie. diagonally (2). Finally, bring the needle back through the canvas via the hole immediately below, ready for the next stitch (3).

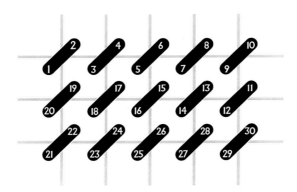

CROSS STITCH

This is a very hard-wearing stitch and thus suitable for rugs, chairseats and cushions. When working in cross stitch be sure to work all the top stitches in the same direction, as in the diagram below. Each stitch should be worked independently, and care should be taken not to twist the yarns. The aim is to produce a clean, crisp stitch. Working the row from right to left, bring the needle up through the back of the canvas (1), down through the canvas (2) and up through the hole directly beneath (3). Take the yarn over the existing slanted stitch and down through the canvas (4), finally bringing it up again at point X ready for the next stitch.

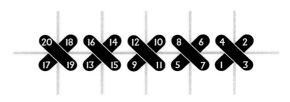

TENT STITCH

A popular alternative to the half-cross is the tent, or continental, stitch. This appears the same at the front, but the yarn is carried diagonally across the back of the work, as shown below, thereby creating a firmer fabric. Tent stitch uses up more yarn than half-cross, so if you choose this alternative, add approximately one third as much yarn again to the specified quantities.

Note: The one golden rule in needlepoint is that when working in tent or half-cross stitch all your stitches should slant the same way. However, this rule has been ignored in many of the Bloomsbury designs!

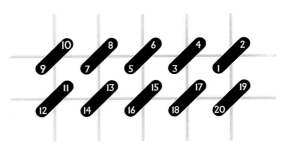

CROSS STITCH OVER THREE HOLES SQUARE

This stitch is worked in the same way as ordinary cross stitch, except that you miss out the hole in the middle. Bring the yarn up through the canvas (1), then take it down through the canvas (2) and up through the next-but-one hole beneath (3). Take the yarn back through the canvas (4) and finally bring it back up at X.

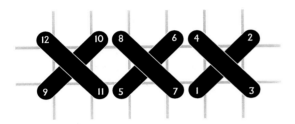

OBLIQUE SLAV STITCH

This stitch is used for quick coverage on the Abstract-pattened Cushion (*see* page 28), and while on the original the stitches have a random appearance, the stitches on the reproduction have been worked evenly. A major advantage of using this stitch is that there is very little wool used up on the back of the canvas The stitch is worked diagonally from left to right up the canvas. The diagram shows the exact sequence used with the needle and the stitch is easier worked than explained. Follow the diagram, bringing the needle up through the back of the canvas on odd numbers and down through the front on even numbers.

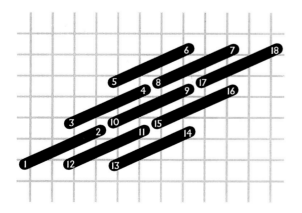

STEM STITCH

This stitch is used to highlight particular sections of a piece, and should be worked on top of the finished needlepoint in black wool. As illustrated in the diagram below, work one straight stitch and then bring your needle back up through the work at the centre left of the completed stitch.

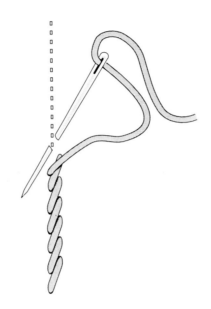

PETIT POINT

For the Abstract-patterned Cushion (*see* pages 28-31), petit point is worked on the double mesh canvas to highlight certain areas. Work as for half-cross stitch, but make the stitches half the size by treating the spaces between the double strands of mesh as holes.

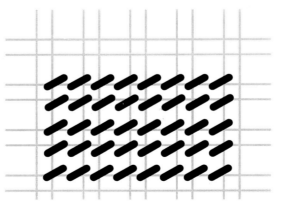

READING THE CHARTS

The charts in this book are not drawn proportionally to the size of your canvas. However, each square represents a hole in your canvas, so colour should be worked as closely as possible on the canvas to the areas allotted to them on the chart. It would also be helpful to take a photostat of the chart you are working on and cross off the rows as you complete them.

TRANSFERRING THE DESIGN TO CANVAS

While designs can be read stitch for stitch from the printed charts, you might find it helpful to trace outlines of the motifs directly on the canvas. To do this, trace your outlines on tracing paper using a black crayon and then place your canvas over your tracing. With a coloured waterproof pen, overdraw the tracing directly onto the canvas.

CHANGING THE SIZE OF THE DESIGN

The simplest way to alter the size of a design is to alter the size of the canvas you select. In other words, for a smaller design use a 12-, 14- or 18-mesh canvas instead of the suggested 10-mesh; for a larger design, use 6- or 7-mesh canvas. Alternatively, you could copy the design on tracing paper and then enlarge it or reduce it at the photocopy shop before transferring the design as described above.

The traditional method is to trace your design and then draw a grid of squares over it, thus defining which part of the design appears in each square. You then select your canvas, draw a grid of an equal number of squares onto it, and then carefully draw in the design outline in waterproof pen, using the squares as a reference.

PREPARING THE CANVAS

You will need the following equipment: masking tape; a waterproof marker pen; scissors; a sheet of blotting paper larger than the canvas.

If you do not intend to use a frame, it is advisable to bind the raw edges of the canvas with masking tape. This prevents the canvas snagging on your wool and also protects your hands from the sharp edges.

As well as transferring your design on to the canvas with a waterproof marker pen (*see* Transferring the Design to Canvas, page 116) you might also want to divide your chart and canvas into quarters or eighths so that at all times you know where you are in your pattern. Similarly, you could run a cotton thread both horizontally and vertically through the canvas to define the middle of the design and in that way provide a point of reference to work to.

Before mounting your canvas on the scroll frame, place it on a piece of blotting paper and draw around it with a pencil. You will need the outline on the blotting paper later on when you are blocking the finished canvas.

JOINING PIECES OF CANVAS

There is no reason why small pieces of canvas cannot be joined together. For example, you may wish to reproduce the rug chart (*see* page 64) a number of times in order to produce a major carpet! To do this, simply overlap the pieces of canvas by at least six holes and stitch your design over both thicknesses. Alternatively, squares of the design can be worked separately and stitched together with strong upholstery thread when the work is complete. When using this second method it is advisable to line the back of the finished piece with hessian, to protect it from heavy wear.

BLOCKING

You will need the following equipment: scissors; a wooden frame or board; upholstery or drawing pins; masking tape; the outline of the canvas on blotting paper (taken during preparation of the canvas); a waterspray or sponge; water; and a hairdryer.

If you have not worked your canvas on a frame, it is essential to block (or stretch) the needlepoint back into shape before making it up into a finished piece. However, even if you have used a frame and it has not distorted I would still recommend blocking, if only to freshen the appearance of the yarns.

Begin by taping the blotting paper to the frame or board. Then place the finished canvas, wrong side up, on top of the paper (moistening it very slightly first if it is badly distorted). Gently stretch the canvas to the outline on the blotting paper and pin it securely to the board, starting at the four corners, continuing along the four sides and using one pin every 2.5cm (1in).

Using a waterspray or a damp sponge, dampen the work thoroughly (on the wrong side) and then leave until it is completely dry. (You can speed up this process by gently playing a hairdryer across the surface.) Once dry, remove it from the frame.

MAKING UP CHAIRSEAT COVERS

The chairseat canvases have been reproduced to the size of the originals. Obviously, these sizes may not suit the chair you wish to upholster. In such a case, your approach should be to make a template by cutting out the exact shape of your required chairseat in brown paper. You can then either increase the size of the plain background area of the design, or change the size of the mesh of your canvas so that you still have enough holes to complete the image but to a smaller overall size.

MAKING UP CUSHIONS

You will need the following equipment: dressmaker's scissors; backing fabric 5cm (2in) larger all around than the finished work; upholstery braid (optional); a sewing machine; a zipper (optional) and a cushion pad.

The original Bloomsbury cushions are made up to a very basic design. They are backed with a heavy woollen fabric and edged in black upholstery braid. In all cases the backing fabric has been cut 5cm (2in) larger all around than the finished work.

With the right sides together, sew three of the sides together by machine. (There is no need to baste down the selvedge on these three sides as it can hang loose inside the cover.) Next turn in and baste down the edges of the fourth side. Then turn the cushion right sides out, insert the cushion pad, and oversew the fourth side by hand. You may prefer to insert a zipper along the fourth side, in addition to adding piping around the edges. However, while cushions can be made up to all sorts of elaborate specifications, too much fuss will destroy the charm of the design.

PREPARING THE BACK OF A RUG

You will need the following equipment: upholstery thread, rubber-based adhesive and backing material – either hessian or rubber underlay.

Having turned back and basted flat the selvedge canvas of the finished needlepoint with upholstery thread, you are advised to stick either hessian or rubber underlay to the back of the rug. Both will give it additional protection from heavy wear and tear and the latter will increase resistance to slipping, especially on a polished wooden floor.

MAKING UP
AS A WALL-HANGING

You will need the following equipment: upholstery thread; a craft knife; wallpaper paste; scissors; lining material; a wooden pole; picture cord and picture hooks.

Having blocked your needlepoint and allowed it to dry thoroughly, turn in the seam allowance on all four sides of the canvas and mitre the corners with a craft knife. Next, size the back of the needlepoint with wallpaper paste to give the piece more body. (Ask your yarn supplier to recommend a brand of paste that will not damage the woollen fibres.)

Cut a piece of lining material 5cm (2in) larger all around than the finished needlepoint. Then machine stitch a 7.5cm (3in) deep strip of the fabric approximately 7.5cm (3in) below the top edge of the lining (on the right side) to form a pocket for the wooden pole. The pole should be between 2.5cm (1in) and 5cm (2in) wider than the needlepoint. Next, press under the seam allowances and oversew the lining to all four edges on the reverse of the needlepoint.

Finally, insert the pole into the pocket, tie picture cord around the exposed ends and suspend on the wall from a picture hook.

AFTERCARE

No matter how many times you wash your hands, work will inevitably get grubby. Provided you have used a waterproof marking pen, there is no reason why you cannot wash your work in very cool water using a washing agent formulated especially for delicate fabrics. Do not squeeze the needlepoint, but leave it to soak for a few minutes before rinsing out thoroughly. Remove excess water by rolling your needlepoint up in a towel, then gently pull it back into shape and leave to dry naturally.

MAKING UP THE BLOTTER

For dimensions of cards and fabric, *see* page 50):
1. Cover sheets of card A and B with the peach-coloured fabric on one side only, but overlapping the other side of the card, as shown. For size of sheets, *see* Materials, page 50.
2. Fold and glue down the top and bottom edges of the blue fabric, so that it is the same length as the cards.
3. Fold the thin strip of blue fabric C in half, lengthways, and press flat.
4. Lay the covered sheets of card A and B right-side-up on top of the strip of blue fabric. Leave 2.5cm (1in) uncovered down the middle of the strip, to form the gusset. Glue in position with rubber-based adhesive.
5. Having covered sheet of card D with the blue fabric on one side only, stitch card D to card B, uncovered sides facing, but leave the middle edges unstitched.
6. Having mounted the finished needlepoint on card E, stitch card E to card A, uncovered sides facing and catching a length of cord at the middle top corner (near the gusset).

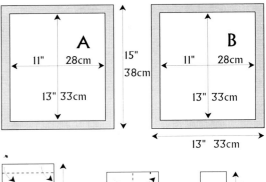

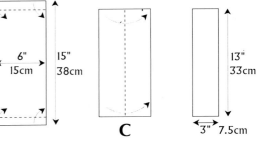

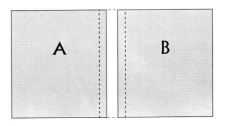

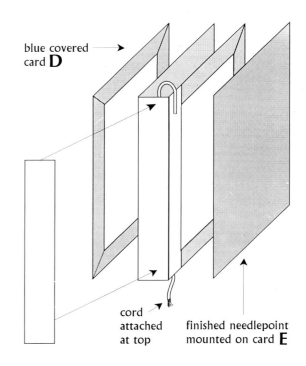

blue covered card **D**

cord attached at top

finished needlepoint mounted on card **E**

INDEX

Page numbers in *italic* refer to the illustrations

YARN AND KIT INFORMATION

Kits for the projects in this book are available
by mail order. The kits contain the correct size
canvas, appropriate yarns and a sewing needle.
A selection of the designs are available as printed
canvases. For full details and prices write to:

Melinda Coss
Ty'r Waun Bach
Gwernogle
Dyfed
West Wales
SA32 7RY
Tel: 0267 202 386

Both Paterna and Appleton yarns are widely
available. If you have any difficulty obtaining
them write to:

UK & Europe   US

The Craft Collection Ltd   Johnson Creative Arts
Paterna from Stonehouse   445, Main St.
P.O. Box 1   West Townsend
Ossett, W.Yorkshire   MA 01474
WF5 9SA   Tel: 617 597 8794
Tel: 0924 276 744

                                    American Crewel & Canvas Studio
Appleton Bros. Ltd.   P.O. Box 453
Thames Works   164, Canal Street
Church St.   Canastota
Chiswick   NY 13032
London W4 2PE   Tel (315) 697 3759
Tel (081) 994 0711

Emu needlepoint stands are available from:
Portfo'lio
30, The Boardwalk
Port Solent
Portsmouth
Hants P06 4TP

PICTURE ACKNOWLEDGEMENTS

The Author and Publisher would like to thank
the following for the use of their photographs:

Courtauld Institute Galleries, London, pages
106-7, 112-3
Tate Gallery Archive (Vanessa Bell Collection),
pages 13, 16 and 19
The Hulton Deutsch Picture Company, pages 10
and 14